CHANGE YOUR MIND

Paramananda

CHANGE YOUR MIND

A Practical Guide to Buddhist Meditation

WINDHORSE PUBLICATIONS

Published by Windhorse Publications Ltd
11 Park Road
Birmingham
B13 8AB
United Kingdom

First published 1996
Reprinted 1997, 1999, 2002, 2005

Printed in Malta by Progress Press Co. Ltd

Design: Dhammarati
Cover illustration: 'Lotus' by Chen Shun, China,
Ming Dynasty, Nelson-Atkins Museum, Kansas City
Photographs © Mark Ludak 1996

British Library Cataloguing in Publication Data:
A catalogue record for this book is available
from the British Library.
ISBN 1 899579 75 3

p.45 'Still Life' is taken from Reed Whittemore, *An American Takes a Walk and Other Poems*, University of Minnesota Press.

pp.136–7 Walt Whitman revised 'Song of Myself' several times. The extract quoted here is from his 1891–2 edition, taken from Walt Whitman, *The Complete Poems*, published by Penguin.

The publishers wish to acknowledge with gratitude permission to quote poems and extracts from the following:

pp.2–3 reprinted by permission of Bloodaxe Books Ltd, from: Miroslav Holub, *Poems Before and After* (trans. Ian Milner), Bloodaxe Books, 1990

p.36 *Japanese Death Poems* by Kaisho, trans. Yoel Hoffman, Charles E. Tuttle Co., Rutland, Vermont/Tokyo 1986.

pp.52–53, 98, 175 *One Robe, One Bowl* by Ryokan, trans. John Stevens, Weatherhill, New York/Tokyo, 1977.

p.151 We quote by permission of the Pali Text Society which owns the copyright in the following work: F.L. Woodward (trans.), *Udana, Minor Anthologies of the Pali Canon* (originally published by OUP), London 1948.

Every effort has been made to trace copyright in the following, but if any omission has been made please let us know in order that this may be acknowledged in the next edition.

p.179 'In Beauty May I Walk' from the Navajo (trans. Jerome K. Rothenberg).

CONTENTS

About the Author

Paramananda was born John Wilson in North London in 1955. From an early age he was curious about Eastern ideas, but it was not until the age of 23, after the death of his father, that his interest in Buddhism was aroused. At this time, the focus of his life shifted from the world of politics, in which he had been active, to more spiritual concerns.

Throughout his twenties Paramananda worked mostly as a psychiatric social worker. He has also been involved in various types of voluntary work, including the Samaritans, drug detox, and more recently in a hospice.

In 1983 he came into contact with the Friends of the Western Buddhist Order and two years later was ordained within the Order itself. Since then he has been teaching meditation and Buddhism full-time in San Francisco and in London, where he now lives. He sees meditation and Buddhism as power tools for both individual and social change, and believes that service to the community is a vital aspect of spiritual practice.

I would like to thank the following for their help and encouragement with this book: David Penn, Jinananda, Susie Slack, and MJ. Also Dhammarati who first taught me to meditate and who designed the book.

Paramananda
San Francisco
May 1996

INTRODUCTION

The Door

In psychoanalytical circles there is a well-known story about a man who is haunted by a recurrent dream. He is trapped inside a room, unable to open the door and escape. He searches the room for the key but can never find it. He tries with all his might to push open the door but it will not budge an inch. There is no way out of the room except through the door which he cannot open. He is trapped and scared. In a session with his analyst he recounts this dream, which has been plaguing his sleep for years. The analyst listens carefully to the dream, paying attention to the details. He suggests that the door might open in the opposite direction. The next time the man has the dream he remembers this suggestion, and finds that the door swings inwards without resistance.

Many people today feel this sense of being trapped, locked inside a life that no longer seems to satisfy them. There is a feeling of quiet despair kept at bay by constant activity or new wonder drugs. Who among us has not at some time felt the need to break out to a new life? Fantasizing about being set free by a beautiful new lover, maybe, or winning the national lottery. Some of us spend our lives waiting; waiting for something to happen that will change our lives. Yet the basic and rather obvious lesson of life, seemingly so hard to grasp, is that happiness is a state of mind, not something that can be taken from others or from the outside world.

All of us seek happiness, but most of us look outside ourselves to find it. We look for it in other people, in our work, in our leisure. As we grow older our dreams slowly fade. We become less idealistic, more pragmatic. We count our blessings and try to be philosophical about the dreams that never came true, or did come true but turned out to be empty of the promise they once held. Mostly our lives settle down into predictable patterns, and we look about wistfully at our broken or empty dreams. In his poem 'The Door', Miroslav Holub, the Czech poet and immunologist, urges us to have the courage to take a fresh look at our lives:

> Go and open the door.
>   Maybe outside there's
>   a tree, or a wood,
>   a garden,
>   or a magic city.
>
> Go and open the door.
>   Maybe a dog's rummaging.
>   Maybe you'll see a face,
>   or an eye,
>   or the picture
>   of a picture.
>
> Go and open the door.
>   If there's a fog
>   it will clear.

Go and open the door.
   Even if there's only
   the darkness ticking,
   even if there's only
   the hollow wind,
   even if
       nothing
          is there,
go and open the door.

At least
there'll be
a draught.

The door that Holub speaks of is the door that opens inwards to reveal our deepest needs and highest aspirations. Meditation is a means of opening that door. When you open it you take the first step into the 'dream' of awakening that has held the imagination of mankind throughout history. It is a dream with no predetermined conclusion; it is an adventure – the adventure of re-creating ourselves, of re-becoming. It is the great human 'myth' of self-transcendence.

Calling it a myth does not mean it is unreal. It means that it is more real; it means we begin to connect with ourselves in a deeper way, to experience ourselves as part of something far greater, far more immense. We step into the whole flow of life. The door of meditation is the door of awareness and loving-kindness, of expansion without a known limit.

Meditation starts with stepping inside ourselves and leads to stepping outside into the stream of life, separation from which is the source of our deepest discontent. When we open this door we never know what we will find – yes, it may well be 'a dog rummaging', but maybe there's 'a garden or a magic city'. Meditation is an opening. At least there will be a draught.

What is Meditation?

Put simply, the art of meditation is the art of being with yourself. It has become almost a cliché to say 'don't just do something – sit there', but this is still something that many of us find very hard to do. What happens if we stop, if we take time out from doing anything other than being aware of ourselves?

There is a celebrated incident from the Buddha's life that poses just this question. The Buddha was once challenged by a king to show that the life of a Buddha was happier than that of a monarch. The king wanted to know how this could be. After all, he pointed out, as a king he had everything that a man could desire: wealth, power, many beautiful wives, while the Buddha had nothing but the clothes he stood up in and a bowl with which to beg for his food.

In reply the Buddha asked the king if he could sit quietly, feeling content and happy, for an hour. The king replied he thought that he could do that. So the Buddha asked if he thought he could sit contentedly for a day. No, said the king, quite honestly, he could not sit for a whole day without becoming restless and discontented. The Buddha then told the king that he, the Buddha, could if he chose sit for seven days and seven nights perfectly composed and blissful, content to do nothing.

In fact, the Buddha led a very full and active life, a life of selflessly helping others. The point he was making was that he did not *have* to do anything in order to feel all right. He was complete in himself, and when he acted he acted out of compassion, not out of a need to assert himself, or to prove himself, or to assuage some feeling of incompleteness.

According to the Buddha's teachings our actions can never be divorced from the state of mind from which they spring. This is the basic idea behind meditation and indeed Buddhism itself. As long as our actions are based upon an inner discontent they will in the long term reinforce the very feelings of discontent we are trying to avoid.

Meditation, however, is a means by which we can become increasingly self-aware, and build up a strong sense of emotional positivity. Based on this foundation we can then act in the world creatively in ways that will help both ourselves and others. All it involves, really, is taking more notice of our mental states and encouraging them in particular directions. Of course, I am deliberately putting it simply; but we need to look at it more closely.

The first thing to realize is that we are often not really aware of what we are thinking or feeling. Or rather, we are not often aware of what we are thinking *and* feeling – because of course we are always feeling, however rational we may think we are. So meditation is the art of getting to know one's own mind; getting to know one's own mental and emotional states; getting to know oneself more and more deeply.

It is on the basis of this self-knowledge that we can begin to encourage the awareness and kindness that will bring a sense of richness and fulfilment to our lives, and from which compassionate action can spring. Slowly we encourage a positive cycle, where mental states of clarity and kindness lead to positive actions in the world, which in turn give rise to further positive mental states. We are all familiar with the concept of a vicious circle. Here is the same principle in its opposite form – a compassionate circle.

Buddhism has a very straightforward way of looking at our mental states. It simply asserts that all our actions, including actions of the mind – our thoughts – have an effect on us. It compares the mind –

our mental states – to a fire. A fire needs to be fed; you have constantly to find fuel to keep it blazing. And the fuel with which we feed the mind, with which we feed the heart, is simply what goes on inside us, the kind of thoughts and emotions that we habitually indulge in, our habits of being.

A fire can burn strong and bright, or it can be dense and dark, with clouds of foul-smelling smoke that choke and blind us. It all depends on the fuel that we use. It often feels as though we have no choice in the matter, that the mind seems to have a 'mind' of its own. But with patience and practice we do have a choice. Through meditation we can gain an increasing sense of freedom and can slowly become masters of ourselves.

This slow process of becoming more aware and learning to encourage what is best in us is the Buddhist path of meditation. It is sometimes called the path of the warrior. This is because it takes courage. It calls for the courage to be really prepared to meet oneself. The *Dhammapada*, one of the earliest Buddhist scriptures, contains the verse 'A man may conquer a million men in battle, but one who conquers himself is, indeed, the greatest of conquerors.'

So the path of meditation is a challenging path. However, it is also a path of great joy and delight. This is because even early on, once we have experienced the fact that we can change in a positive way – that we are not just victims of the circumstances we find ourselves in – we feel a great sense of relief. We know that even if it takes many, many years to undo the negative habits of one's own particular vicious circle it is possible to do so. There is great hope and joy in knowing that we have started out on the path of transformation.

When we come to the practice of meditation we all come with our own unique history. We bring our own particular strengths and weaknesses to our practice. We bring ourselves. This in a way is the key to meditation; a bringing of what is there – ourselves. But what does it mean to bring all of ourselves to the meditation cushion?

So often in our lives we find ourselves playing a role, just showing a part of ourselves. At work you might be the responsible employee, at home the loving parent, with friends the good listener or the witty conversationalist. Rarely do we completely let all our various roles just drop away. But when we sit to meditate we have an opportunity to let all that go. Our first task is just to experience ourselves, experience whatever is there. We can at last let drop any idea of performing a role. One might feel that one is not a spiritual sort of person or that one is no good at things like meditation. Well, we bring all that sort of thing along as well.

For most of us it takes quite a while to get all of ourselves there on the cushion. Sometimes we are very good at bringing the parts of ourselves that we like while at other times we just bring the parts we dislike. We all do this, and it takes a gentle persistence to get *all* of us there. But once we are there, warts and all, beauty spots and all, we find we have a tremendous energy to work with.

Sometimes this is called riding the dragon. It can be frightening, but it is also invigorating. We begin to feel more fully alive, more ourselves. Dr Edward Conze, in his *A Short History of Buddhism*, remarks that it is only in cultures which honour the dragon that Buddhism has flourished. In a way it's the same for us. We need to learn the dragon's name, learn to look at the hidden aspects of our own life, and then we will find that the power of the dragon is no longer fearful, but a great energy in our favour.

Anyone reading this book is going to be looking for something. To some extent we are not happy – or at least not as happy as we would like. This is the place we all start from. In Buddhism this feeling is called *dukkha*. *Dukkha* is a word from Pali, the Indian language of the early Buddhist scriptures, and it is normally translated as 'suffering', but this is probably a bit misleading. Pali words cannot often be translated without their real meaning getting lost, as they come from a culture with a rather different outlook on the world.

Dukkha could perhaps be better rendered as 'unsatisfactoriness'. We might not like the idea that we are suffering. We might feel uneasy with the idea, given that we live in a relatively affluent culture, with enough food on the table and so on. But dukkha isn't really suffering in that sense. It is suggested that it derives from a term meaning an ill-fitting wheel. So the image is one of riding in a cart when one of the wheels is loose on its axle – it's an uncomfortable ride.

Of course sometimes it might feel as if the wheel isn't just ill-fitting; it seems to be missing altogether – and our ride really is painful. But even when things are going along quite well we still have this feeling of dukkha; we still don't feel completely at ease. Either we are worried about the future or we just don't really enjoy what is around us. We are over-active and restless, or else, perhaps, we lack energy, never quite getting it together. All these kinds of feelings – as well as the more powerful feelings of distress we sometimes have – are dukkha.

Buddhism is known as the path leading away from dukkha. It is not a religion in the normal sense of the word. It is rather a kind of training aimed at bringing about the end of dukkha. It offers us techniques and ideas that help us to lead more satisfying lives.

A very important part of that path is meditation, and in the Buddhist tradition there are many types of meditation practice. In this book we are going to be concentrating on two of the best-known forms of meditation, central to all traditions of Buddhism and taught by the historical Buddha 2,500 years ago. They are, therefore, well tried and tested.

Roughly speaking, meditation techniques can be divided into two kinds, known as *samatha* and *vipassana*. These are Pali terms and are most commonly translated 'tranquillity' and 'insight'. The term *samatha*, or tranquillity, refers to calm, emotionally positive states of mind. *Samatha* meditation encourages the gradual integration of the psyche. It brings together one's disparate sub-personalities into a unified whole, so that the mind is no longer divided against itself and one is able to act with energy and focus.

Vipassana or 'insight' refers to the direct comprehension of 'reality', free from the distortions of greed, hatred, and delusion. So insight meditation is the form of meditation that aims at bringing about this direct 'seeing' into reality. We will be taking a closer look at the idea of 'insight' later on.

Traditionally the two practices we will be concentrating on fall into the first category. They are regarded as *samatha* meditations. Sometimes when people hear this they think 'Oh, I don't think I'll bother with them – I would rather gain insight: that sounds a lot more exciting.' But as we shall see, it is of great importance that we first establish a calm and clear mind. Anyway, this categorization shouldn't be interpreted too rigidly. In fact most so-called *samatha* meditations can also be used as insight practices. It is not a matter of which particular meditation practice we do so much as the attitude with which we do it that determines whether or not it includes an element of insight. I hope we will begin to see how these simple meditation practices, once we are confident in their use, encourage insight as well as lead to clarity and calmness.

First, we will be taking a look at a practice called the Mindfulness of Breathing. This is concerned with developing clarity of mind, and with becoming more aware of ourselves and the world around us. The other meditation I will describe is called the *metta bhavana*, another

Pali term. *Metta* can be translated 'universal loving-kindness' and *bhavana* means 'to cultivate' or 'to develop'. So it is the cultivation of universal loving-kindness, and it is concerned with becoming increasingly emotionally positive and kinder, towards both ourselves and other people. Together, these two practices give us a powerful and direct means of affecting our lives, helping to make us happier and more aware.

But before we start on the meditations themselves we need to consider the body and the posture we adopt for meditation.

one

THE BODY

The Diamond Throne

If asked, most of us would probably say that meditation is concerned with the mind. We might even hint that it is a kind of mind control or a way of putting oneself into some sort of a trance. In fact, to begin with anyway, meditation concerns not the mind so much as the body, although this is really just a way of talking, as you can't separate the two. They are not two separate systems operating together, but two ways of talking about the one system which is us.

However, it is useful to think that meditation begins with the body if only to counteract our tendency to think of the mind, in its limited sense, as something that functions quite separately. We will perhaps be clearer about this if we think of meditation as being concerned simply with the quality of awareness. Awareness is a quality of the whole of us, not just of the mind or the body. If you watch a skilled potter working on a wheel, you see that their awareness is concentrated in their hands. When you watch a skilled actor, you find that the emotional meaning of the performance is revealed in the use of the body as much as in the spoken words.

Many of us seem to inhabit our heads rather than our bodies. It is as though all our energy is in our heads, and our bodies are rather elaborate vehicles for our brains to get about in – like sci-fi aliens with giant heads on underdeveloped bodies. There is also the opposite extreme, of total identification with the body, seeing the body as the ultimate repository of our sense of who we are. We can, it seems, go to either extreme: devaluing the body, or becoming obsessed with its superficial appearance.

In meditation, we are not concerned with either of these extremes. We are looking at the body in an altogether different way. We are trying to re-inhabit our bodies. We want to bring our awareness into our bodies, to rebuild a relationship with our physical selves that is characterized by a sensitivity like that of the hands of the potter, and an awareness of the emotionality of our bodies such as the actor might have.

One of the best-known symbols of Buddhism is that of the Buddha seated in meditation. This image can help to give us a sense of what we are trying to move towards when we meditate, and it conveys quite a lot about the spirit of meditation. It is an image found throughout the Buddhist world and increasingly in the West. The Buddha's body expresses a sense of profound relaxation and alertness. It is still and composed, but at the same time vibrant. It seems alive with subtle energy. We see in this image that meditation is something that happens as much in the body as in the mind. I want to spend a little time talking about the image of the meditating Buddha before moving on to deal with the more practical aspects of posture.

The life of the Buddha makes a wonderful story. Very briefly, it is the story of a boy born into great luxury as the son of a local king in northern India, who becomes aware of the suffering inherent in human existence, of the impermanence that seems to vitiate even the most favourable circumstances of life. He is groomed by his father to be a ruler, but develops an intense desire to understand the source of human suffering, *dukkha*, and to find a way for himself and all others to be freed from it. Accordingly he leaves his homeland and lives the life of a wanderer, going from one spiritual teacher to the next. After many years of hardship he finally gains Enlightenment. He spends the rest of his long life teaching the path to Enlightenment that he has discovered, to all that would listen.

The Buddha's life serves as a kind of blueprint or pattern for Buddhists, because it is as much in the events of his life as in his teachings that the wisdom of the Buddha is revealed. Here I am concerned with the image of the prince on the verge of breaking through to Enlightenment, but it is well worth reading a fuller account of the Buddha's life, as the story can be a source of great inspiration, whether or not one thinks of oneself as a Buddhist.

Prince Siddhartha encountered great difficulties in his attempt to find an answer to the unsatisfactoriness of human existence. He brought himself to the brink of death in trying to liberate his 'spirit' from his body by means of the severe ascetic practices that were popular at the time. He became so weak that he nearly drowned in a shallow river whilst bathing, and this experience brought the realization that such self-mortification was of no use. He saw that unless he changed his ways he would very soon die without having found any solution to the fundamental problems of existence.

He resolved therefore to regain his strength and try a different approach. This new approach came to him out of a memory of his childhood. Once as a young boy he had been seated under a tree, watching his father plough a field, when he quite spontaneously entered into a state of great bliss and contentment. It now occurred to him that such a state might form the basis upon which a higher understanding could arise. So, having eaten, he seated himself under a tree, composed his body and his mind, and brought his powers of concentrated awareness to bear upon his examination of the human predicament.

It is at this point that, according to Buddhist mythology, there arose a figure called Mara, 'the evil one', who gathered together all his forces to try to prevent Siddhartha from becoming the Buddha. On a psychological level we could say that Mara is the personification of all the forces within our psyche that are resistant to change, and want to keep things as they are.

I am sure we are all familiar with at least some aspects of ourselves that are resistant to change, even if consciously we feel quite clear about what we would like to do. The prince was on the verge of going beyond the normal self-centred aspects of his own being, so it is not surprising that the opposite forces within him should rise up in a last desperate attempt to resist such profound transformation.

In Buddhist art, Mara's forces are depicted as a vast army of strange and furious beings hurling all kinds of missiles at the prince, while he sits composed and undisturbed. As the rocks and arrows come close to the prince's body they are transformed into beautiful blossoms and fall harmlessly around the majestic figure. After the failure of his attack, Mara tried a different approach to turn the prince's mind away from the task it was resolved upon. Mara tried to instil a sense of doubt in his mind by questioning his right to be seated on the 'Diamond Throne'.

Here Mara is referring to the place that Siddhartha has chosen for his meditation. According to Buddhist myth, all Buddhas gain Enlightenment on the same spot, and this is said to be the central point from which the whole universe unfolded. Now this doesn't mean you have to go to India in order to meditate properly: in a sense, the Diamond Throne is created wherever someone sits in deep meditation. It refers not to a physical space, but to an unshakeable attitude. When you sit with complete composure you sit at the centre of all things; you create a centre of stability within the constantly changing chaos all around you.

So Mara challenged Siddhartha's right to seat himself on this spot. In reply the prince extended his right arm and touched the earth with the tips of his fingers – a gesture of the hands known as the 'earth-touching *mudra*.' This is an image of the Buddha that is very often depicted in Buddhist art.

What happens next is quite wonderful. The goddess of the earth rises up out of the ground and testifies that the prince is indeed rightfully seated on the Diamond Throne, by virtue of his own great effort. She testifies that she has seen Siddhartha, throughout many life-times, develop to the point of perfection all the positive qualities of the human being – qualities of generosity, patience, energy, kindness, and awareness. At this testimony, Mara is completely undone and flees in dismay.

We might well wonder what this episode of calling the earth to witness, pivotal as it is in the life of the Buddha, has to do with us as individuals just embarking on the path of meditation. If we allow it to speak to us, we will find that it resonates with our own situation, at the very beginning of our own personal spiritual quest. We too need to call the earth to witness. We need to feel that when we take up our meditation posture we are, at our own level, occupying the Diamond Throne.

Every time we sit down to meditate we are involved in the supreme human task of transforming the forces of Mara into the positive energies of the earth goddess. We are engaging in the process of evolution. As human beings we are the result of millions of years of evolution and development, from the time that the universe first took form. When we sit, we sit with the whole of this history behind us. In us, the process of evolution has become self-conscious. This is a truly remarkable thing. We have the opportunity to take evolution forward: as individuals, we can transform the seemingly blind, chaotic forces of nature into an increasingly concentrated power of self-awareness, clarity, and loving-kindness.

This might sound a little grand and overwhelming, when perhaps all we want is to learn to relax a bit, to calm down and enjoy life more fully. However, if we can engage those aspects of ourselves that reach out to go beyond what we now are, we will find that our lives become far richer. We will feel, perhaps for the first time, that our life is of real significance and meaning.

I'm not suggesting that we become puffed up and inflated with our own spirituality – we will soon find that such attitudes are the food of Mara. But we should take ourselves seriously. Buddhism teaches that all human beings are capable, through their own efforts, of Enlightenment. Even if we have only a glimpse of what such a state of being might be like, it is a wonderful thing just to feel that we are moving towards it, however long it might take us to achieve.

This attitude of sitting as though on our own Diamond Throne is developed through our meditation posture. This does not mean we have to sit perfectly in 'full lotus' position. It means sitting with confidence and a clear intention. It means learning to experience our body as a gift that comes to us out of inconceivable aeons of evolutionary development, and to feel that in this very body we can realize the highest expression of life.

Principles of Posture
Different schools of Buddhism have different ideas about which posture to adopt for meditation, and its importance, but essentially what we are trying to achieve is a posture that is comfortable and

alert. Of course it is good if you can sit comfortably in a full lotus position, but unless you have done many years of yoga, or something similar, it is unlikely that you will be able to do so. You have to take into account your age, physical condition, and so on.

I like to use the word 'comfort' when talking about posture, not only because it means sitting at ease, but also because it has an interesting derivation. 'Com' means 'with', and 'fort' means 'strength', so 'comfort' means 'with strength'. Sitting comfortably also means sitting 'with strength'.

There are three general modes of posture to choose from. However, if you have particular health problems you may have to work out your own solution to them – whilst bearing in mind the basic principles of good posture.

There are two distinct ways of sitting on the floor, or of course you can sit on a chair. I have heard many horror stories about people on retreat who are told that the only way to meditate is by sitting on the floor, and who spend the whole retreat struggling with unnecessary physical discomfort. There is nothing wrong with using a chair if this proves best for you.

Sitting on the Floor

You can sit either in some kind of cross-legged position or astride a few cushions. For many people sitting astride is a better option as you don't need to be as flexible in order to do it. You should choose this position if you are not able to get the underside of the lower legs easily on to the floor in some form of cross-legged position (fig. 1).

When you sit astride cushions you will normally need to be quite high off the ground – high enough not to put undue pressure on the lower legs or the ankles. You will soon find out if you are too low because it will hurt. And here is a good time to say very clearly that pain should *not* be endured during meditation. A certain amount of discomfort is a common experience when we are still quite new to meditation – after all, most of us probably haven't sat still on the floor since we were children, if ever. But pain is our body's way of telling us we are damaging it. So listen to it.

When you sit astride the cushions your legs and feet should point straight back. They should at least not be too splayed out. Your ankles should not be bent so that your feet stick out to the side. The rest of the posture is the same either way you sit, so let's move on to the cross-legged position.

In general, I would tend to favour the cross-legged position unless you are distinctly more comfortable with one of the other options. You can sit in 'full lotus' or 'half lotus', or just with one leg resting in front of, or on top of, the other.

These positions are never, of course, entirely symmetrical because one leg has to be on top of or in front of the other. So if you are going to do a regular meditation practice it's a good idea to alternate the relative position of the legs. It sounds more complicated than it really is!

Whether you sit straight or not is determined by the angle of your pelvis, and this in turn is dependent on the height of your cushions. It is my experience that most people tend to try to sit lower than they need to. All I can say is that it really isn't more 'spiritual' to only use one cushion. Experiment a little with the height of your seat to determine what feels right.

What you are trying to achieve is a cushion height at which the pelvis feels upright, which will mean that the weight of the body feels as though it is falling directly down through the pelvis into the floor. In other words, the weight is not being taken by the legs. If you are too low your back will have a tendency to bow out, whilst if you are

Fig. 1 Kneeling astride cushions

*Fig.*2 Cushions too high

*Fig.*3 Cushions too low

Fig.4 Sitting cross-legged

Fig. 5 Sitting cross-legged, side view

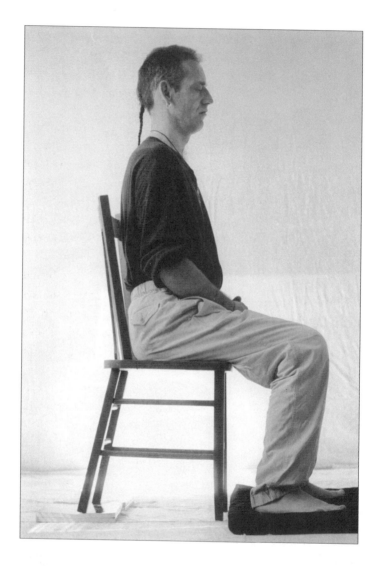

*Fig.*6 Sitting in a chair

too high, the opposite will happen – the back will arch in (figs.2 & 3).

The idea of a straight back is rather misleading, as the spine is naturally curved and to force it to be straight is both impossible and undesirable. It is more that the back should feel naturally and easily erect, not collapsed in the lower back or forced into a 'ramrod' posture.

We need to have a sense of patience and sensitivity when we work with our posture. We might have sat in a rather slumped manner for many years, and to expect a 'good' posture right off is unrealistic. But if we get the height of our cushions right – and this can mean quite small adjustments sometimes – we should be able to get a fairly upright posture without too much trouble.

The type of cushion we use is important. It should not be too soft, like a pillow. If you are unable to find firm cushions, one option is to roll up pillows quite tightly to make them firmer. If you decide to take up meditation it is well worth investing in some good cushions made for the job. It's the only expense involved in having a regular practice and it really does help.

Some people find they get on better on a meditation stool or bench, which should be fairly easy to find these days. The advantage of a bench is that it provides a firm sitting surface – you can use a thin cushion to provide a little padding. The disadvantage is that you are stuck with the same height, so make sure you know how high you need to be before you buy one.

Once you have the base of your posture right the rest tends to fall into place. Your arms need to be relaxed, supported either on the legs or in the lap, with the elbows kept quite close to the body. I like to wrap a blanket around my waist and tuck my hands into the top of the blanket. If your hands hang too low you may find that the weight of your arms pulling at the shoulders produces middle to upper back pain after a while. Your hands need to be in a position that allows your shoulders to be relaxed and your chest open.

Your head should be very slightly inclined forward but not to the extent that you are constricted in the back of your neck or throat. Note that it should be your head that inclines forward, not your neck. The neck should be as upright as the rest of your spine.

Sitting on a Chair

It is OK to use a chair for meditation. It should have a fairly firm seat. It sometimes helps if the back legs are raised up just a little by means of, say, a phone directory or two. The resulting slight tilt will make it easier to maintain an upright posture without strain. Your feet should be flat on the floor, which will both help to relax your legs and provide stability and contact with the ground. Generally speaking, the back of the chair should not be used for support. If you are tall, try to find a chair with legs long enough to allow your knees to be a little lower than your pelvis. The rest of the posture is the same as for sitting on the floor.

Getting the Body Right

We all have habits of the body as well as the mind. For example, we might tend to hold one shoulder higher than the other, or our head to one side. This means it is not always easy to tell if we are sitting well. It can be useful, therefore, if someone else has a look at how you sit and gently adjusts your position. If you normally hold your head slightly crooked, it will at first feel lop-sided when it is adjusted to a better position. Posture is an important element in meditation and it is not just a matter of finding the correct posture then forgetting about it. We will need to work with our posture as part of our meditation practice.

There is a definite link between the state of our mind and our posture. This is why some forms of Buddhism put so much emphasis on the body. For example, in the Zen tradition they say 'get the body right and the mind will naturally be concentrated'. And if we can work with the mind by working with the body, the converse is also true. As we become more concentrated the body will often adjust itself. We might feel our shoulders relaxing or some other part of the body where we tend to hold tension just easing off and allowing the body to straighten up and relax. As we become more experienced in meditation we will discover that even very subtle physical adjustments can make a big difference to the way we feel when we sit, as well as to our mental states.

While everyone's body has its particular limitations, it can, with sensitivity, patience, and a good posture, become a source of great energy and pleasure within our practice. We might also find that meditation is a means by which we can slowly come to a different relationship with our body.

Experiencing the Body
Our attitude towards our own body is an important element in our attitude towards life. It is well known that a lot of people feel dissatisfied with themselves as a result of seeing their own bodies as objects. In extreme cases quite severe mental suffering can be caused by people who compare their own objectified bodies with unrealistic media and advertising images of what the body is meant to look like.

Our culture has produced a dramatic split between the mind and the body – we tend to overvalue either the one or the other. And if we do not experience ourselves as an integrated whole, one consequence of this is that we associate certain emotions either with the body or with the mind. In some cases people are completely unable to feel certain emotions that they associate with the body.

So some people can be attracted to meditation because they are rather alienated from the physical aspect of themselves. They have the idea that meditation will allow them to disappear into an abstract world where the body is no longer experienced. And it is true that in certain highly concentrated states our experience of our body may become quite attenuated. However, in order to achieve these states we have to pass through others where our body awareness is very acute.

Furthermore, these states have their origins, at least in part, in the ability to experience the body as a source of pleasurable feelings and sensations. Mental bliss arises out of bodily rapture. Within the meditation practices we will be spending quite a bit of our time working directly with the body, and we will see that it is the body that provides the basis for meditation.

Body Meditation

Awareness of the body is the foundation for the practice of developing mindfulness, and for the cultivation in meditation of positive emotion as well. The body is our fundamental reference point in meditation. It is by maintaining a sense of our bodies when we meditate that we keep the practice in the realm of concrete experience, rather than drifting off into an abstracted or alienated state of mind.

Being aware of the body also helps us to tune in to, and stay in contact with, our emotional state. In meditation, the awareness of the body provides the context for the particular meditation practice that we are doing. That is, it provides a broad, experiential reference for the focus of the practice. We will be taking a closer look at this idea of breadth and focus later on.

All meditations should be preceded by a short practice of the kind that follows, though as a rule it probably doesn't have to be quite so protracted. Generally, we won't need to take more than a few minutes over it unless we find that we are feeling rather disconnected from our body and our emotions.

Being aware of the body means directly experiencing the sensations, feelings, and emotions associated with it. When we first try to experience ourselves in this way it is not at all uncommon to find it quite difficult. Many people are rather disconnected from their bodies, taking notice of them only when they do not feel right. The body can experience pleasure as well as pain, but often – unless this pleasure is quite intense, as in sexual activity – we hardly notice it at all.

So we want slowly to try to become sensitive to the more subtle sensations occurring all the time in our bodies. For a moment, close your eyes and just become aware of your palms, fingers, and the back of your hands. You can probably feel a constant flow of sensation in them. You can feel whether they are warm or cold. You might well have the experience of energy, the body's vitality, flowing through them. Because hands are packed with nerves they are a good place to start coming back to, for a simple, direct experience of ourselves. Certain parts of our body are much less abundant with nerve endings; they do not need to be as wonderfully sensitive as our hands. Nevertheless we can still learn to bring our awareness to them.

Although we are trying to have a direct experience of ourselves, rather than just an idea, this does not mean that the mind is of no use in helping us towards this experience. The imagination in particular can be of great help in beginning to get us back in touch with ourselves. One exercise I sometimes use in meditation classes is to ask students to select a category – animals, say, or plants or types of weather – anything that comes to mind will do. Then I ask them to sit quietly – or lie down if they prefer – and take their awareness through the different parts of their body, associating each part with the category they have chosen. You can start either with the feet and work upwards, or vice versa. So, for example, if you started at the top with types of weather as your category, you might feel that your head was foggy or misty or, perhaps, bright and clear....

This probably sounds a little wacky but it can be fun, and it should help us begin to take an interest in what is happening inside. Interest really is the key to starting to make progress in meditation. We have to stimulate an interest in what we are doing or we will find our minds just go elsewhere.

Something else I do is give people paper and lots of coloured pencils and ask them, after a body meditation, to draw their experience; not to draw what they look like, but rather what they feel like. The drawing that comes out of this exercise might bear no resemblance to the body at all; it might be completely abstract (in an artistic sense) with swirling colours, light and dark patches, areas of movement, and heavy, static areas.

There are many such exercises one could do, such as writing poems about what your body feels like. The point is to stimulate an interest, even be a bit playful. We don't need to become all solemn and heavy about what we are doing. Much better if we can enjoy it. We are taking up meditation in order to be happier, so the cultivation of a playful interest is a good way to start. All these simple exercises are ways of 'mapping' the body. The meditation that follows below is another.

Don't skimp on preparing properly for this meditation. Choose a time when you will not feel rushed. Find a relatively quiet place in your home, turn the answerphone on. Read through the led meditation a few times, so that you have a good sense of its form and content. Alternatively, you might like to do this exercise with a friend, in which case they can read it to you. Take your time setting up your posture, making sure that you have enough cushions and that you will be warm enough. Don't have the room too warm, though, or you will tend to fall asleep.

Body Meditation: *a led practice*

Once you have a comfortable position, close your eyes and allow your face to relax. Take a couple of deeper breaths. As you breathe in, feel your chest gently open. No need to puff it out – you're not on parade. Just allow it gently to open up a little. Then as you let out the breath, relax the shoulders, easing them down and back.

See if you can take your awareness down into the parts of your body in contact with the cushion or the chair. Have a sense of contact with the ground. If you are sitting on a chair, check that your feet are planted flat on the floor. Feel the weight of your body bearing down on the ground, feel the solidity of the body.

Now become aware of the soles of your feet, allowing them to soften and relax. Try imagining that you are drawing up awareness from the ground, up into your body. Slowly allow this awareness to move up through your feet into your ankles and lower legs. You might like to imagine this awareness as a kind of light, or a feeling of warmth in your body.

Let the muscles of your lower legs relax, allowing them to soften and become heavy. Notice any sensation in the part of the body where your awareness is, but do not force anything. If you don't feel much that's fine; just notice what is there.

Letting the awareness move up into your knees, imagine a sense of space in your joints, then move the awareness into the large muscles of your upper legs. Allow your muscles to fall away from the bone under the soft force of gravity.

Broaden your awareness to include your buttocks, pelvis, and genitals. Experience this whole area filling with soft, warm awareness. If you notice any slight 'holding' of energy, which is quite common in the buttocks, try to let the awareness soften it.

Now gather your attention at the base of your spine. Do not try too hard: we cannot force awareness without tensing up. Just gently bring your mind back when it drifts off. From here we are going to trace the line of your spine slowly up through the body.

Bear in mind that the spine is well inside your body, rather than on the surface of your back. It is quite hard to get a sensory experience of the spine, so we need to use our imagination a little. But by this I don't mean just inventing some sensation that isn't there. It's more a matter of a kind of openness to very subtle sensation.

Trace the gentle curve of your spine up through your body, through the lower back, the middle back, and between your shoulders up to where your spine meets the base of your skull. This is quite high up, about level with the top of your ears.

Once again, see if you can gather your awareness at this point. Ease the muscles at the base of your skull – imagine them letting go, the muscles relaxing like a fist unclenching. Your head isn't going to topple over if you forget to hold it up – we'll find that it can balance very nicely by itself. Imagine that your head can move perfectly freely and is just poised on top of your spine. You might want to adjust your head slightly to achieve this quality of feeling.

Now, locating a sense of the top of your spine, take your attention back down the spine to its base. Try to hold both these places in mind – the base and top of your spine. Imagine these two areas being infused with light, a warm, soft light, and that these two points of light are very gently – more just a tendency than an actual movement – easing apart. One is drawn towards the earth, the other towards the sky. Try to hold this image for a few minutes; these two points of light very slowly moving apart, like two stars in the night sky imperceptibly drifting away from one another. See if you can soften the two ridges of muscle that run down either side of your spine. Imagine that as these muscles soften, your spine is released, and these two points of light can ease further apart.

Allow your shoulders to relax a little more. Then begin to take your awareness into the top of your arms and slowly down towards your hands, collecting it in your palms and fingers. Use the sensations in your hands to get a sense of the vitality of your body.

Now bring the awareness into your belly – another area where we often find the flow of energy held up. Then slowly up into your chest. Feel the movement in your chest, your rib-cage gently opening to accommodate the breath. Have a sense of the breath opening your chest.

Move the awareness up into your throat, and then into your face. Soften your face a bit more, taking time to feel the sensations there. Become aware of the shape of your skull – allowing the skin of your scalp to become soft – then extend your awareness to the crown of your head. See if you can feel any sensation at this point.

Become aware of the touch of the air against your face. Feel how very sensitive your face is; notice the temperature of the air, and allow your face to soften against the air.

Now without any particular effort, notice the process of breathing that is taking place. As you draw down the air into your body imagine that the air is saturated with awareness, like a soft mist of tiny water particles. So as we take the air in, we also draw down awareness.

Follow the breath down into your body, down until you become aware of the movement of your belly as you breathe in and out. Let your breath be calm and gentle. Don't force it down. Notice your belly as it moves to accommodate the breath. Allow the breath to soften your belly from the inside out. Notice the movement in your chest, at the sides of your body, in your back; feel the whole of your rib-cage gently moving with the breath.

Breathe in a sense of spaciousness; the space outside you becoming space inside you. Gently gather your attention around the area of your heart. Just sitting and breathing, be aware of any sensations in the area around your heart. Allow the breath to create space around your heart, space for how you feel, for your emotions.

Just breathing, being aware of your body, your breath, being aware of your feelings, let the feelings come and go in a sense of spaciousness, just as you let the breath come and go. Stay with this as long as you feel comfortable, just being with yourself.

Then feel your connection with the ground once more. Allow yourself to be aware of the room in which you are sitting and any outside noises, and in your own time allow your eyes to open, bringing the practice to an end.

This exercise is both a 'body mapping' and a relaxation. It is an excellent preparation for meditation, or it can be used on its own to help us relax and calm down. In this exercise we use the imagination to help us come into contact with our body and our feelings.

Sometimes we might like to try simply sweeping the body with awareness from feet to head and back again, without imposing any ideas at all – just bare sensation. This can be very effective when we have some experience of being more aware of our bodies, but I think to start with it is probably more useful to engage the imagination.

Try to imagine your awareness having a colour. Or ask yourself what each part of your body feels like, letting an image come to mind. Do use the imagery association method I suggested before. It can be a lot of fun and rather interesting to relate different parts of the body to different examples of a particular class of image – animals are great to do!

You can, if you like, work out other ways of becoming more aware of yourself within the meditation. Do not be afraid of experimenting. To begin with go with what feels right. Just remember not to force the attention. There may be areas of the body you find it hard to be aware of, but if an area feels dull or dark do not force yourself to be aware of it. Simply be patient and bring your common sense and an attitude of care and kindness to whatever you find.

two

THE MINDFULNESS OF BREATHING

Mindfulness

We are now going to take a look at one of our two meditation techniques: the Mindfulness of Breathing. First I want to discuss mindfulness itself, then we will move on to look at the meditation designed to help us cultivate this quality.

Probably the most widely employed method of developing some degree of mindfulness – at least in England – is fishing. Fishing is apparently the most popular participatory sport in England, and I remember as a child spending many happy hours sitting by the canal waiting for the float to dip. Now that I'm a Buddhist, I wouldn't want actually to catch fish – I'd have to follow the example of the famous Zen master who fished without a hook. However, fishing does serve as a good analogy for mindfulness. Someone fishing is often in a beautiful, peaceful setting, for quite a while, in a calm, relaxed state of mind, with a definite object of focus for the mind in the 'float' bobbing on the water.

I am sure that one reason fishing is so popular is that it creates the conditions necessary for a very enjoyable experience we call mindfulness. Mindfulness arises very simply and spontaneously when we are calm and relaxed, with a definite object of concentration for the mind. It is therefore a natural state we all experience at least sometimes. In fact, there is always some element of mindfulness in our experience unless we are in some kind of very het-up state. What we want to do, then, is consciously cultivate this naturally positive quality of mind.

For a moment, imagine doing something you really enjoy, and that you have all the time in the world to do it. What is the quality of feeling that this evokes? It probably feels quite bright and expansive. It is not at all similar to what we think of as 'concentration'. It is very different from the sort of forcibly fixed attention we might employ in order to complete a rather demanding but unexciting task. It doesn't have the contracted and hard feeling we perhaps associate with concentration.

Mindfulness is a bright and expansive mental state. Sometimes it is said that a concentrated mind is a happy mind, and this happily concentrated mind is a relaxed type of concentration. It is mindfulness. Mindfulness includes a strong element of interest and pleasure. There is a sense of expansion to it, a sense of opening up rather than narrowing down. At the same time, there is a sense of clarity and purpose. The mind is balanced, poised, and full of creative energy.

In meditation we consciously cultivate this state, so that it becomes much more likely to be available to us in daily life. You could say that this mindful state is the mind's natural state, in that it is the state of mind from which we can act most effectively. It is the mental equivalent of the physical elegance of a cat. The mind is relaxed and flexible, ready to engage fully and positively with anything.

When we are sitting quietly in meditation our mindfulness is carried in our posture as well as in our mind, as we saw in the previous chapter. But if through meditation we exercise this capacity of the mind, we will also begin to experience it more and more in the rest of our lives. We might even find that chores which we previously performed reluctantly and mindlessly become enjoyable.

It has become a bit of a cliché in Buddhist circles to talk about washing the dishes mindfully. Washing the dishes has become a sort of archetypal mindfulness exercise for Westerners, like pounding rice has for Japanese Zen monks. But there is an important point here, which is that activities we tend to think of in rather negative terms provide ideal conditions for the development of positive mental states.

This brings us back to the idea of a self-perpetuating cycle of mental states, which can be either positive or negative. That is the nature of 'conditionality', the truth at the very core of Buddhist thought. It is a simple idea with profound implications, and in terms of our mental states and actions it works as follows. What we feel, our state of mind, provides the conditions that give rise to what we do, and how we do it – what we think, what we say, and what we do physically. At the same time, what we do and how we do it acts on our state of mind by providing the conditions giving rise to what we feel and how we think. So this is how we live, and it is the cultivation of awareness that allows us to break into this cycle and change a negative cycle into a positive one. In Buddhism this is the main purpose of developing mindfulness.

One way to get a feeling for the quality of mindfulness is to sit down in your favourite spot, put on a piece of music that you really enjoy, and give yourself over to it. (I don't know if this will work if you are a heavy metal fan, but I hope you begin to get the idea.) Mindfulness is the quality of mind we experience when we are absorbed in something, particularly something beautiful, and it is also closely associated with the creative dimension of the mind.

Sadly, many of us experience such a clear and expansive state of mind only very rarely. I have met people who feel they have to go back to their childhood in order to get a sense of what is meant by mindfulness. So much of our lives is taken up with things we do not really enjoy, things we feel we have to do – or should do. Even in our leisure time we can find ourselves in a bar or club, supposedly having a good time, and wondering what is the matter with us and why we are there. We can find ourselves desperate to enjoy our free time without knowing quite how to do it. The cultivation of mindfulness is the basis for a happier life; a life that carries a sense of meaning and richness. Without this quality the best we ever experience is a kind of forced happiness, a kind of 'smile – you're supposed to be having fun' approach to life.

I have stressed that mindfulness is a natural quality of the human mind. But it still needs to be actively cultivated, because so much in our lives pulls us away from it. It seems to me that television is a symbol of modern life: the average American television is on for seven hours a day. We live in a culture of relentless downloading of information in which we have little or no real interest. Even if we think we are capable of keeping it out, we have to expend a lot of energy to do so, and still it seeps in under our defences. For most of us it is vital that we give ourselves time out from all this, that we consciously cultivate the opposite quality of mind.

However, we can find that if we are stressed or worried, we will not be able to experience this state even under apparently ideal conditions. A friend of mine recently returned from a trip to the desert. It was a wet spring and the desert was in bloom. Anyone who has seen this will know it is a breathtaking sight. She knew it was a breathtaking sight, but felt quite numb to the beauty. She returned with the realization that she had to do something about her life because she was losing her ability to appreciate her surroundings.

Mindfulness is this ability. It is not a cool, hard attentiveness to things, but a warm appreciation. If you look at some of the paintings of the Pre-Raphaelite school of the nineteenth century, you see this great attention to detail, together with a vibrant subject-matter, pulsing with colour and energy. If we can imagine the state of mind capable of such attention to – and appreciation of – its subject, then that is what we are after.

Unless we are lucky enough to spend most of our time doing what we really care about, it is likely that this quality of mindfulness has become a little dulled. It needs to be exercised and nourished. And the best way to do this is to practise becoming aware of our breath.

This might at first seem a long way from the blooming of the desert and the wonders of art. The breath probably doesn't seem immediately interesting or beautiful. But there are many reasons why one's own breathing is a great place to start the process of reawakening this wonderful quality of mindfulness. It is true that mindfulness responds to what is out there in the world through the mediation of the senses; but its source is not to be discovered through the senses. Mindfulness allows us to appreciate, to enjoy, to take a real interest in things. However, although it is nourished by these enjoyable things, it is not produced by them.

We have probably heard of the great Zen painters who can render all the delicate, tensile grace of a blade of grass with a single swift stroke of the brush. The story is that these painters would spend hours just looking, becoming more and more aware of their subject, becoming as one with their subject. It was only when they had achieved deep mindfulness of their subject that they would, quickly and effortlessly, execute the painting. Often these brush paintings are extremely simple – literally just a mark or two.

The same quality can be found in good Zen poetry. (There is a lot of bad Zen poetry around, which imitates the form but misses the inimitable spirit.) Nearly always the subject is simple. There is a feeling of directness. It seems that what is being conveyed is not so much an image, or an idea, but rather a direct experience of the subject or event. Japan has a tradition of 'death poems', poems written shortly before death. Here is the death poem of the Haiku poet Kaisho, who died in 1914 at the age of seventy-two.

> Evening cherry-blossoms;
> I slip the inkstone back into my kimono
> This one last time.

Traditionally in Japan great care is taken over the preparation of the ink by the poet. Part of the beauty of a poem lies in the brush strokes that form the characters, so the consistency of the ink, made from an inkstone, is very important. Kaisho knows he will not be writing another poem so he places the inkstone into its container and then into the folds of his kimono. The essence of mindfulness lies in this ability to experience directly. As Wallace Stevens, the American poet, puts it: 'Not ideas about the thing but the thing itself.'

The Mindfulness of Breathing

The breath is part of us and at the same time something to be directly experienced. It is very simple, but at the same time our experience of it can be tremendously fulfilling and rich. It can become a direct experience of life ebbing and flowing within us. This awareness of our own selves is the best foundation for a greater awareness of all that is around us.

The Mindfulness of Breathing is the bedrock of all meditation practice. Other more exotic practices, such as, say, the visualization of archetypal figures embodying spiritual virtues from the Tibetan tradition, are powerful exercises on their own level, but without a firm foundation in basic awareness they are little more than pleasant distractions.

If we really want to make changes in ourselves, we need first to be aware of where we are starting from – what we are now. And this awareness is developed pre-eminently by the practice of mindfulness. All forms of meditation need a strong element of mindfulness or we will simply become distracted. Without mindfulness we might achieve a pleasant enough state of mind, but we cannot really call it meditation.

I love the Mindfulness of Breathing. After many years of regular practice it is still the meditation I most enjoy. It has a simplicity and directness I have not found in any other practice. All we have to do is be aware of our own breath. Nothing could be simpler. Yet it is a practice to last a lifetime, becoming richer and richer over the years, and contributing in a very direct way to the rest of our lives.

Before we actually do the practice I want to talk a little more about the breathing. The breath is perhaps the most consistent thing in our lives, starting when we are born and ending when we die. I think of the breath as a kind of thread running through my life. It seems to me that it is the breath that connects one moment to the next. This act of breathing we share with all higher forms of life. It is, in a sense, life itself, and I sense that my breathing links me to everything else that lives. Sometimes when I sit with my breath I feel I am aware of the whole world breathing; it is as though the earth itself breathes. To me the breath has a wonderful richness; it is both a symbol of life and life itself.

The breath also has a property that is very useful if we wish to become more aware of ourselves. It can function to connect us with our emotions. The breath mirrors our emotional states; it is affected by how we are. By just being aware of the breath we find that we also become more aware of the body and of our emotions. This is a very important part of the practice of mindfulness – awareness of the body and the emotions. We will also find that trying to stay with the breath makes us notice with far greater clarity what it is that we spend all our time thinking about!

Enough for the moment on the virtues of the breath; let's take a look at the structure of the practice itself.

If you were to sit in a good posture and gently bring your attention to your breath, bringing the mind back to the breath when it drifted away – you would be practising the Mindfulness of Breathing. It is that simple. But although it is very simple in theory it can be quite difficult in practice, so it is structured in a way that leads us from easier exercises of mindfulness to more challenging ones. It has four distinct stages, which I shall describe briefly before elaborating with a guided meditation.

The practice should be preceded by some time spent setting up a good posture and becoming aware of the body. This can be achieved by doing a short body meditation such as that described in the last chapter. To start with, the whole meditation, including the preparation, should be kept fairly short, say about fifteen to twenty minutes. Make the four stages roughly the same length.

It is far better to do a short period of meditation that you enjoy than trying to meditate for longer and becoming uncomfortable and distracted, so that your meditation just seems like hard work. More experienced meditators often find that forty to fifty minutes is a good length of time, but this is too long for most beginners. If you enjoy meditating you will find that you naturally extend your periods of meditation as your body gets used to the posture and you learn to become absorbed more easily.

Once you have settled down a bit and taken in how you are feeling through being aware of your body, bring your attention to the breath. It is important to realize that this meditation is not a breathing exercise; we are not trying to breathe in a 'spiritual' way, or do some kind of yoga exercise. We are just letting our breathing be as natural as possible. If you find that your breath changes, fine – it is a living thing – but don't deliberately alter it; just stay with it.

Stage One

At the end of an out-breath count 'one'; after the next out-breath count 'two'; after the next, 'three', and so on. Continue counting silently after each out-breath until you reach 'ten'. Then start again at 'one' and carry on as before. In both this stage and the next, remember that you are meant to be mindful not of the counting, not the numbers, but the breath. The counting just helps you to realize when your attention has wandered, which might be quite often at first.

Stage Two

This is different from the first stage only in that you change – or make as if to change – the point at which you count. You still count between the exhalation and the inhalation that follows, but you now count just before the in-breath, so you are anticipating the next breath rather than marking the breath you've already taken. Though you might feel you are counting in more or less the same place, this stage actually feels quite different from the first.

Stage Three

Drop the counting altogether and simply sit with as full an awareness as you can of the sensation of the whole breathing process.

Stage Four

Focus on the point where you first experience the air as you breathe in. For most people this will be just inside the nostrils (assuming you are breathing in and out through your nose, which is best unless there is some reason, like a heavy cold, that makes this difficult). This is normally quite a subtle sensation but you should not have too much trouble being aware of it once you have deepened your attentiveness with the first three stages. If the third stage is like watching the ocean breaking on the shore, the fourth is like watching the ocean breaking over a rock.

This sensation is, of course, coming and going. And it might be even more subtle going out than going in, because the air is now much the same temperature as the body. So the sensation will wax and wane, but try to keep your attention at the same spot. Unless you become very concentrated you will still be aware of the main body of the breath, so I tend to say to students that it is more a matter of placing an emphasis, or the weight of your attention, on this spot, rather than trying to keep out the broader awareness of the breath.

So much for the bare bones of the practice. Now here is an example of a guided practice I would use when teaching students. As with the body meditation, read the description through a few times and then give it a try, or get a friend to read it to you as you do it. Make sure you will be free from interruptions, and find somewhere quiet. Fifteen to twenty minutes is a good length of time to start with – keeping the four stages about equal in length.

The Mindfulness of Breathing: *a led practice*

Set yourself up comfortably in your meditation posture; don't rush. Make sure you are sitting up straight, your seat is the right height, and your legs are not taking the weight of your upper body. Make sure your hands are supported. Check that your head feels balanced firmly and easily on your neck.

Take a couple of slightly deeper breaths, and allow your body to relax. Feel your shoulders ease, your face soften. Feel a sense of letting go of the day, and just coming into the here and now.

Experience the contact of your body with the floor. Imagine giving the whole of your weight to the ground, just letting the ground support you. Try to have a sense of the weight of your torso falling directly down through the pelvis into the earth.

Imagine that the more completely you give up the gross weight of your body, the lighter the body feels and the more easily energy can move in the body. So there is a feeling of the weight of your body being held by the earth, and at the same time you can feel the subtle energy in your body rising upwards. There is this opposite yet complementary movement of weight and energy in your body.

So let your body settle into its posture, allowing your shoulders to relax, checking your belly and buttocks for any holding of energy … relaxing your face. Have a sense of your body becoming quiet, becoming still … of the space that your body takes up … and of the space around your body.

Now without any special effort, start to take notice of the breath. We don't need to grab at it – it isn't going anywhere. It is always just there, waiting for us patiently to notice it. So we begin to notice it.

Follow it down into your body, into the space inside your body. Notice how your body responds to the breath, the movement low down in your belly, the gentle expansion and contraction of your chest at the sides and back.

So as you sit with this breath coming and going be aware of how you feel. Let the breath bring you in a simple and direct way to yourself, your feelings, at this moment. What is the tone of your being – light or dark, happy, sad, dull, excited? Just have a general sense of your self, your basic emotional state. Acknowledge your feelings.

Come back to the breath, coming and going. There is plenty of room for your feelings in the breath; allow them, like the breath, just to come and go.

Now begin to count the breaths, counting at the end of each out-breath, just marking the breath. Count to yourself, make the counting just strong enough to stay with the breath. If you lose count, start again at 'one'. It doesn't matter. The breath is still there, waiting for your attention. Just sit with the breath in this way for a few minutes.

Now we are going to make a small change. The breath is just the same, coming and going, but now we count at the beginning of the breath, just before we draw the breath in. So we are anticipating the breath by an instant. Count 'one' – breathe in, breathe out; count 'two' – breathe in, breathe out.… Let the breathing be easy, just follow it.

Keep your body relaxed, your face soft.… Not straining to stay with the breath; just coming back to it whenever you feel your mind moving away … just using the counting to help you keep an eye on your mind. If you lose count, start again at 'one'. Never mind how it happened, just start again. So you are counting in sets of ten, just staying with the breath for a few minutes.

Now let the counting fade into the breath; let it go. Here you are, just with the breath; there is nothing else in the whole world that you need to do just now. Just follow the breath. It does not matter if you lose it – it is always there, waiting for you to come back to it.

Just like watching the great ocean upon the shore, coming and going, feel the breath wash over you, and then withdraw. Feel the whole of the breath, each breath becoming the next. The great tide of your breath inside you – feel it in the body, filling the body, bringing life and energy into the body. Just you and the breath, just the breath, coming and going.... Stay with the breath for a few minutes.

Now, while experiencing the whole of the breath, begin to notice the first sensation you experience as you draw in the breath – where the breath first 'breaks' against your body. You're looking for a subtle sensation in your nostrils or at the back of your throat – wherever you first feel the breath as it enters your body.

Keeping your face relaxed, begin to gather your attention around this point, noticing more and more this detail of your breath. It is a constantly changing sensation, so it cannot be pinned down. If you try to take hold of it you will lose it. Attend to it, appreciate it, let it go. Don't force your attention but look for a sense of enjoying the sensation as it comes and goes with the breath. Spend a few minutes enjoying this sensation.

Now come back to the whole of the breath. Be aware of your body, be aware of the ground beneath you. Slowly become aware of the room around you and any sounds inside or outside the room. Have a sense of the outside world, and in your own time allow your eyes to open and your body to move.

A New World

The regular practice of the Mindfulness of Breathing introduces into our lives an increased sense of spaciousness. We will find that our mind feels less busy. The less busy our mind is, the closer we are to the truth; the more active our mind is with chatter, worry, or fantasy, the less aware we are of what is actually going on, both inside us and around us in the world.

On a meditation retreat people often have the experience of walking out of the meditation room into what seems like a whole new world. Suddenly, everything seems so alive and vibrant. Because the habitual chatter of the mind has stopped, or at least greatly lessened, you are a lot more aware of the beauty of the world around you. In a sense, the world is the same as before – it reflects your mental states back to you as it always does. But if you change your own mind, then the world changes also.

So mindfulness can bring a new dimension to all we do. One of the most blissful experiences of my life took place on a retreat during which we were practising a lot of mindfulness. I had come out of the meditation room and collected my sleeping-bag which had split open. I sat in the sun, on some stone steps that went up the outside of the old stone barn that was our meditation room, and sewed up my sleeping bag. I can't sew very well, but I sat there sewing up this bag as carefully as I could, and I was in bliss. Normally, I would have been annoyed that my sleeping bag was falling apart; I would have been frustrated at what a bad seamster I was. But no. I just sat there in the sunshine, in the beautiful Welsh countryside, taking care to sew as well as I could, and it was one of the highlights of my life.

Mindfulness opens up a new world. Even in the city it reveals the beauty all around us. Instead of seeing the same old drab facts, we appreciate the precious and unique reality to be found everywhere. We look with new eyes, we feel, touch, taste – even smell – afresh. The world is renewed to us; we stop taking for granted that we 'know' what things are like, what other people are like, and see them the way they really are, as unknowable and therefore real. We begin to hear what people are really saying to us, instead of hearing what we expect or what we want to hear. We notice the quiddity of things.

There is a poem I like very much, 'Still Life' by Reed Whittemore, that seems to me to capture this near magical quality of mind....

I must explain why it is that at night, in my own house,
Even when no one's asleep, I feel I must whisper.
Thoreau and Wordsworth would call it an act of devotion,
I think; others would call it fright; it is probably
Something of both. In my living-room there are matters I'd
rather not meddle with
Late at night.

I prefer to sit very still on the couch, watching
All the inanimate things of my daytime life –
The furniture and the curtains, the pictures and books –
Come alive,
Not as in some childish fantasy, the chairs dancing
And Disney prancing back stage, but with dignity,
The big old rocker presiding over a silent
And solemn assembly of all my craftsmen,
From Picasso and other dignities gracing my walls
To the local carpenter benched at my slippered feet.

I find these proceedings
Remarkable for their clarity and intelligence, and I wish I
might somehow
Bring into daylight the eloquence, say, of a doorknob.
But always the gathering breaks up; everyone there
Shrinks from the tossing turbulence

Of living,

A cough, a creaking stair.

Of course the world is not all beauty and kindness. It is also full of 'tossing turbulence', and we have to struggle to see the world with 'clarity and intelligence'. When we become more aware we also become more aware of the suffering around us. Here I do not mean just the awful things that happen in 'other' countries, but also the day-to-day unhappiness of so many people.

I have often sat on the London Underground returning from a meditation class, just looking around at the people. Most of them seem to me quite down-trodden, squashed by life. Few seem able to make any sort of human contact, simply to look one another in the eyes. A close friend told me about a time when he was returning from his first retreat on a bus. He became convinced that some terrible disaster had happened while he was away because the people on the bus appeared to be in a state of shock. It was some time before he realized that nothing had happened; it was just a normal bus-load of passengers.

Meditation opens us a bit more to this level of everyday suffering. Where before we chose not to see the distress in the faces of others, now we see it. Therefore it is important that along with the cultivation of mindfulness we also cultivate a positive emotional outlook, robust enough to take in the real suffering in the world without being overwhelmed by it. It is important that we should be able to respond realistically and creatively to our surroundings. The Metta Bhavana helps us do just that.

three

LOVING KINDNESS

The Metta Bhavana

The *Metta Bhavana* is sometimes called the development of universal loving-kindness. It is one of a set of four meditations known as the *brahma-viharas*, which means something like 'abodes of the gods'. So we could say that the practice of this meditation and its three companion meditations (of which I shall say a little more later) are designed to put us in the same frame of mind as the gods.

I should mention that the Buddhist idea of gods is rather different from the one we are probably used to. To start with, there are quite a lot of them. Furthermore, being a god is not a permanent condition. A human being, according to traditional Buddhist teaching, can become a god by being reborn in a god-realm; this happens if they have been particularly good! But they will not remain a god for ever; at some point they will be reborn in a different realm, of which there are many.

The point about the *brahma-vihara* meditations is that they help us to experience positive and enjoyable mental states that are equivalent to the mental states of the gods. The Metta Bhavana is the foundation of this set of meditations. The others, which are concerned with the development of compassion, sympathetic joy, and equanimity, are, in a sense, aspects of this basic practice. So the Metta Bhavana is really the most important of the four, and the place where we need to start.

The Metta Bhavana may seem at first sight very different from the Mindfulness of Breathing, but the two complement each other very well. Even if we prefer one of the meditations to the other, which most people do, we will find that practising the one enriches our experience of the other. In the end, they are both about developing awareness. Let's see if we can get a handle on what is meant by the word *metta*, and then we will look at the structure of the practice itself.

The Pali word *metta* is often translated 'universal loving-kindness'. Sometimes it is rendered simply as 'friendliness' or, less often, 'love'. I rather like the least common rendering – 'love'. It has drawbacks in that it usually refers to romantic or sexual feelings, which few of us in our culture need consciously to cultivate. But despite these connotations, for me it has a certain directness and strength that makes it seem appropriate.

Bhavana is another Pali word, and it means 'cultivation' or 'development'. So this meditation is about the cultivation of metta. The idea that we can cultivate some emotions rather than others goes rather against the grain in Western society. I get the impression that most of us think that whilst we may learn to control the expression of our feelings through discipline or strength of character, we are more or less stuck with the basic way we respond to things emotionally. Buddhism does not take this view. The Buddhist view is that whilst our basic emotional attitudes are quite deep-seated, it is within the reach of all of us to change, if we know how. We just have to make a consistent effort.

So this meditation is concerned with the cultivation of positive emotion. More than that, it is about establishing in ourselves a basically positive attitude towards ourselves and others. Whilst we are often aware that our moods change from day to day, or even from hour to hour, we can also probably sense a kind of background emotionality. We all have our ups and downs, but it is clear that different people deal with these inevitable fluctuations in very different ways.

The Metta Bhavana is concerned with giving us a positive emotional foundation or background to our lives. To begin with, our practice of this meditation is in great part a kind of investigation of our emotional life. It is an application of increased awareness, or mindfulness, a sense of clarity, to our emotions. It is not a matter of controlling them. It is a slow process of getting to know ourselves; learning to acknowledge who we really are; then encouraging the more expansive and warmer aspects of ourselves.

I remember very well the first time I heard this meditation taught. I was on my first meditation retreat. At the time I worked as a psychiatric social worker and I tended to see the world in psychological terms. That is, I adhered to the view that we are only able to alter our basic emotional patterns through long and exhaustive therapeutic intervention, and that even then it is more a matter of learning to adjust to those basic emotional patterns than fundamentally transforming them.

When the teacher had introduced the meditation, which he did in a simple straightforward way, I thought 'No, this can't work!' But I was also filled with a sense of excitement: 'Suppose it does work! Can Buddhists have been wrong for 2,500 years?' Well, many years later I can say that no, they were not wrong, although it must be said that the effects of the practice are not necessarily instantaneous. Nor do I find it an easy practice – whereas I took to the Mindfulness of Breathing like a duck to water. However, I do feel it is a wonderful meditation and, perhaps because I have had to work rather harder at it, I have gained great benefit from it. And I am still filled with a sense of excitement whenever I teach this meditation.

This is as good a time as any to underline the fact that meditation is neither a cure-all nor a quick fix. We have spent all our lives – many life-times according to the traditional Buddhist view – acquiring our mental and emotional habits. If we are going to change them significantly it is going to take time and practice. Buddhism is realistic in this way – neither pessimistic nor optimistic, but realistic. And this is one reason I feel it can be trusted. Change is indeed possible, but it requires time and effort.

We are all unique. Who we are is a complex combination of many factors – our biology, our race, our family, the social context of our lives, and so forth. From the point of view of meditation, it does not matter much what weight we give these various factors; they have all played some part in what we have become. The point is that we are a product of conditioning.

This conditioning has been going on not just for this life-time. Whether or not we accept the Buddhist idea of rebirth or re-becoming, it is still true that as human beings we are the product of the whole evolutionary process. And whether or not we accept the full implications of the central Buddhist truth of conditionality, most people would probably accept its general thesis, which is that all phenomena arise in dependence on conditions; everything is the result of a complex set of conditioning factors.

We too are the product of conditions – laid down by our circumstances and the habits of mind we have developed over the years. And we can now go on to change the conditions we set up, if we choose. We are, to the degree that we are aware, responsible for ourselves. It is this gift (and curse) of self-reflective consciousness that defines us as human, and that gives us choice. As long as we remain only dimly self-aware we can avoid having to confront those choices. If on the other hand we want to be more aware, more alive, we have to make those choices; we have to start the long process that leads to liberation.

While in this vein I might as well risk putting you off the whole idea of meditation. If you take up meditation at all seriously, you are introducing into your life a powerful force for change. Some parts of us do not want to change. Change can be frightening, and we can never say with any certainty where it will end. We are therefore, in a sense, inviting conflict. Furthermore, change is not just some kind of head-trip; it has real consequences in the real world, in our world.

We will not be just the same kind of person, but a bit more positive, a bit more aware. Over time we may become quite different, and this will have repercussions. This is a kind of health warning I try to remember to give to people learning meditation. Meditation is an adventure, and the very nature of adventure is uncertainty. After having meditated for a few years people often find that their lives have turned upside-down. I have not, I should say, met anyone who has regretted it – but be warned. Well, I feel I have done my duty as a responsible meditation teacher now, so let's get back to the Metta Bhavana.

In the last chapter we saw that mindfulness is not an emotionally neutral state. It is in itself a clear, bright, and positive mental state. But at the same time we need to address our emotions more directly.

Later, we will be looking at the idea of 'insight' (in the sense of insight into the nature of reality) in some detail. But it is worth mentioning here that this insight – which is the goal of Buddhist practice – is not a dry affair. It is an affair of the heart at least as much as the intellect. What would happen if we suddenly saw everything as it really was? It is rather probable that we would be overwhelmed by the experience.

The problem that confronts us is that we are deluded. And this delusion is not so much intellectual as emotional. It is our emotional need to try to fix ourselves and the world around us. We know in our heads that everything about us, and in us, is in a constant state of flux. But in our hearts we continue to cling desperately to the things we love – or even to the things we hate. We want things to stop changing, we want permanence in our lives. The fact that no such permanence exists anywhere threatens the very core of our sense of ourselves.

So there is little point in being more aware of all this reality if we lack the positive emotional basis from which we can respond to it in a creative and joyful way. In order to take on the fact of impermanence, and therefore rid ourselves of the suffering which comes from clinging to a false view of reality, we have first to cultivate a strong sense of loving-kindness or metta – towards both ourselves and others.

It is this positive emotional base coupled with the clarity of awareness that prepares us for the arising of insight or wisdom. Insight is a deep penetration into reality supported by loving-kindness and mindfulness. This wisdom is not to be found somewhere out there; it cannot be learned. It is a direct experience of ourselves and of our true nature.

If you speak delusions, everything becomes a delusion;
If you speak the truth, everything becomes the truth.
Outside the truth there is no delusion,
But outside delusion there is no special truth.
Followers of the Buddha's way!

Why do you so earnestly seek the truth in distant places?

Look for delusion and truth in the bottom of your own
hearts.

So according to Buddhism there is no special truth to be found
outside of oneself, outside of one's own nature. The finding of this
truth does not depend on intelligence or exceptional talent of some
kind. It is simply a matter of being aware of oneself in a deeper and
deeper way. This is all that we need to do. But to be fully aware of
anything we must have a real interest in it, we have to want to
understand. You could even say we must have a passion to understand.
Our emotions have to be involved, we have to have a sense of care,
concern, and sympathy.

The basis of metta is this sort of concern towards ourselves. We
have to want to be happy! Our happiness has to be based upon love
towards ourselves, for if it is dependent upon the love coming to us
from others it will sooner or later break down. We have to learn to
like ourselves for what we are, not in comparison with others. When
we have positive feelings towards ourselves it becomes much easier
then to like others; we are not threatened by them, we wish them to
be happy as well.

To have sympathy towards ourselves means to be honest – to seek
the truth – within a context of understanding and love. We have to
be able to recognize our faults and to acknowledge that we make
mistakes. We don't just shrug them off and get on with making more;
we try to see them clearly and at the same time keep a perspective,
recognizing that we are much more than our faults and mistakes, that
we also have the capacity to love, to be creative, to give and to change.
If we develop metta towards ourselves we will be able to see our

failings within a broader context and they will not overwhelm us. The same will be true of our attitude towards others.

The Metta Bhavana is a very simple practice. There is nothing difficult about it. It becomes difficult only when we are looking for something that is not there. If we are trying to work with delusion it will be painful. If we want to feel great compassion when in fact we are fed up and depressed, we are creating a gap which will be filled with frustration and pain.

If, on the other hand, we start from where we are, from feeling fed up, we will feel good that the meditation has helped us to shift those feelings, even if only a little bit. We will experience a sense of change, a sense that we can work with our feelings. In fact, when we start from a position of honesty, we open up the way for real change to take place, and sometimes we will find that this change can be quite dramatic.

The practice is divided into five stages. In each stage we try to direct a feeling of metta towards a different person (or persons, in the case of the last stage).

Stage One
As we have seen, the ability to feel metta towards others is based on, or is dependent on, the ability to feel metta towards ourselves. This is therefore where the practice begins. In this stage we try to cultivate a sense of metta towards ourselves. Sometimes this can feel quite awkward – if we have been brought up to feel that caring for ourselves is selfish.

In fact, if you think of someone you know who is selfish, it is, I think, unlikely that they will strike you as having a deeply loving attitude towards themselves. Selfishness has its roots in a feeling of impoverishment. We feel that everyone else has it better than us; that it's a dog-eat-dog kind of world and we are going to get ours.

Generous people normally seem quite content; they like themselves; they have an inner richness and do not feel depleted by giving to others. Here I am not so much talking about material generosity, which is to some degree dependent on material wealth, and can even be a substitute for real generosity. I am talking about people who make us feel they have time for us, who will go out of their way to be helpful. Generosity is a very important part of the Buddhist path, because it is the outward expression of metta. In this sense it is a kind of barometer of mental health. So to cultivate metta towards oneself is the first step towards being less selfish.

In this practice it is important not to think in terms of imposing metta. It isn't a matter of just overlaying our old emotional patterns with a surface film of loving-kindness. The meditation is working towards making deep changes in those patterns, not covering them up. So it has to be done on the basis of how we really feel, not how we would like to feel or how we think we should feel.

We have already discussed this a little in relation to the body, but it is well worth repeating: we need to be as much in touch with ourselves as we can before we begin the practice. Again, a short body-awareness exercise will help us. However, this does not mean raking around looking for trouble. Let sleeping dogs lie, as the old saying goes; they will awaken when they are ready and we can take them out for a walk then.

So we want to try for an honest, direct experience of how we are at the time we undertake the practice. We want to leave aside ideas about who we are, and concentrate on what we actually experience. Once we feel we're aware of our general state of mind we can begin to think in terms of encouraging metta towards ourselves.

We need to contact a sense of wishing ourselves well, even if we are aware that other feelings are also present. So we begin to work with whatever positive feelings we already have. We are not sitting here like a hanging judge. We have a concern for ourselves as towards a loved friend. We are being open-hearted towards ourselves, and tender. It is with this attitude that we work with what we find in our experience. We begin to nurture what is positive, to give energy to it. We do this by showing an interest in it. No feeling is too small for our interest.

It is as if your child has brought home a painting from school. You do not tell her it is not a very good painting. You can see she is very pleased with it, she has put her heart into it. So you too can see that it is a wonderful painting: it is wonderful because it is a positive expression from her heart.

Any positive feeling we have is wonderful in the same way. It is worth our attention. So we allow ourselves to enjoy it. Anything we can appreciate in our experience of ourselves we should be aware of and encourage in this stage.

A much-used way of doing this is simply to say a few encouraging words towards oneself: 'May I be well, may I be happy, may I be free from suffering, may I make progress.' The point of this is, of course, not just to say the words but to encourage a feeling or emotion of kindness or warmth towards oneself. This approach works well for some people, but there are many other methods we can use, which I will discuss later on.

Stage Two

Now we bring to mind a good friend, someone whose company we enjoy. It is said that it is best to choose someone who is about your own age, who is still living, and of the same sex. To be on the safe side

I usually suggest you choose someone of your own sex towards whom you do not have any sexual feelings. These conditions help to keep this stage of the practice as clear-cut as possible, and most of us will more easily and naturally feel an affinity with friends of our own sex.

So we bring to mind this person. Don't spend too long trying to think of exactly the right person – it's not as critical as all that. I normally just say to myself 'a good friend', see who pops up, and go with them – unless it's clear they don't fit in to this section.

Try to hold this person in mind. Some people find visualization easy, so this is a good method to employ to help keep the person in mind. If on the other hand visualization is a bit of a mystery to you, as it is to me, there are plenty of other things you can do to evoke this friend. I find I am good at calling to mind people's voices, and I often listen for, rather than look for, my friend.

You are trying to hold this friend in your awareness, so if you drift off, this is the point of reference to come back to. Once you feel you have established some degree of contact with your friend, you can wish him or her well. Again you might use words, or you might just feel warmth or love flowing towards them. Of course, you can make a conscious effort to stimulate such feelings, but you can't force them, so don't try to do that. Just be open to what is actually happening. These feelings might be strong or faint; you might feel nothing at all, or even quite inappropriate feelings. The important thing is just be aware of what is happening.

If you feel you are completely losing your way, take a deep breath and come back to yourself, then start again. Often this stage will be fairly easy; you have chosen someone you care about, so just bearing them in mind should be enough to set going a flow of warmth towards them.

This is a very important stage of the meditation, as it begins to encourage us to spend time with positive feelings, and allow them time and space to grow. How often do we give ourselves this chance to enjoy our feelings of friendliness, to relish our appreciation of someone else? We tend, for some reason, to indulge negative feelings a lot more often. If you think of someone who has recently upset you, you will find, most probably, that you spend a great deal of mental energy on this person – a lot more than you do on feelings of friendliness.

Having said that, metta is rather more than just wallowing in the special friendships we may have. Metta is not a 'sticky' thing, so the work in this stage involves letting go of the friend, allowing them to be happy for their own sake, not for ours. We have to try to let go of our own expectations of them, our own need for them. This is not necessarily all that easy, so we need to be patient with ourselves.

Stage Three

In this stage we bring to mind a different person, this time someone that we could call a 'neutral' person, someone we have no strong feelings towards, one way or the other. It might be someone we work with but have never really got to know, or it might be someone we often see in our locality; it doesn't matter too much. What we are trying to encourage here is an expansion of our normal emotional range, a broadening of our emotional awareness to include those who do not have a direct impact on our lives.

We are trying to experience the same well-wishing towards this person as we do towards our friend. So we are encouraging the beginnings of a basic reorientation of our whole emotional life; a movement away from an emotionality based in a self-referential attitude towards an attitude that is far more expansive and open. I am sure that at some point in our lives we have all experienced metta from a stranger – an act of friendliness free from any selfish motivation. It might be as simple as a smile, or help when we need it.

A word I often use when describing this stage is solidarity. We are encouraging a feeling of solidarity towards others, not because they have a direct effect on our lives, but simply because they too are alive. We know, if we use a little imagination, that these neutral persons share with us the same range of emotions; they have their hopes and fears, their joys and pains, just as we do, and it is on the basis of this recognition of our shared humanity that we find the desire to wish them well. I hardly need to point out what a different world we would find ourselves in if we all took the time and trouble (perhaps I should say time and pleasure) to cultivate such feelings towards each other.

Stage Four

We now make a move into enemy territory, that is to say, we bring to mind a person who would normally provoke in us rather unfriendly feelings. We bring to mind an enemy, or at least someone we find difficult or irritating. This is a very interesting stage of the meditation to teach, as it tends to provoke strong reactions from people. These range from denying there is anyone they dislike, to honestly stating that they do not want to wish such a person well, as this would seem hypocritical.

To those who say they don't have anyone they dislike in their life I sometimes suggest they bring to mind a member of their family. This normally gets a laugh of recognition. The problem here is that we tend to think that if we are a 'nice' person we shouldn't have such feelings. But it isn't a matter of what we should or shouldn't have; it is just a fact that these feelings are part of our lot as human beings. It is very unlikely that we don't entertain any negative feelings at all towards anyone. It is much more likely that we do not acknowledge these feelings in ourselves because we think they are bad.

This is important, because it takes a lot of emotional energy to hold down these more negative feelings, and while our energy is being employed to do that it is not available to us for more useful things. It is relatively easy to transform energy, but that energy must first be available.

I have worked with many deeply depressed people, and very often one of the first signs that the depression is beginning to lift is an upsurge of anger. This is an extreme example, but the principle holds true in more subtle forms. It is as if these feelings are the crudest expression of our emotional energy. The crude ore has to be extracted before the process of refining it can begin. So don't worry about having these negative feelings – they are the raw material for metta. Nor is there any need to worry if it takes us a little while to free up some of this energy. Once again, don't force it. Trust in the practice.

As for the other extreme, people who frankly admit to strong feelings of hatred or dislike, but do not see why it is in their own interest to work with these feelings – I like to tell them the analogy for hatred in traditional Buddhism. Hatred is likened to picking up a burning log or coal to throw at your enemy; quite possibly you will miss, but you can be sure that you will burn yourself. Hatred is not something we can direct at others without it having a seriously unpleasant effect on ourselves. So even if at first one cannot honestly find an altruistic motive for working with these types of emotions, there is a good enough reason of self-interest to get us going.

However, this is the stage where there may be some risk of falsifying what you actually feel. Do not expect great waves of over-whelming love to flow from your heart. It is very nice if they do, but don't imagine they are the norm. It is more likely that you will drift into revenge fantasies; one moment you're sitting there trying to experience loving-kindness, and the next you have an axe in your hands!

If something like that happens, try to see the humorous side of it. Go easy on yourself; just take a breath, centre yourself, and try again. If it's really too much, pick someone else; maybe you will have to work up to dealing with your *bête noire* gradually. Even when you see the uselessness of hatred it is still difficult to give it up. According to Buddhism, negative attachment is as strong as, if not stronger than, positive attachment. It is often harder to give up what we hate than what we love, so take it easy.

In this stage it's particularly important to stay in touch with what is going on in your body. Usually, negative feelings, as well as positive ones, have a physical component. This is of great help to us because it gives us another means to work with what is happening. We shall take a closer look at this later, but for now just think about keeping the body relaxed but alert. It's really quite hard to feel anger when you are physically relaxed and open.

Just do your best to wish this person well. You can reflect that there is probably a lot more to this person than the negative aspects you pick up on. You can also bear in mind that – from a Buddhist point of view at least – trying to wish this person well really means wishing their happiness, and in particular their spiritual well-being. If that person were happier, more aware, kinder, would you still find them so difficult?

Note that in this practice we are wishing people well, not kidding ourselves that everyone is really OK, when clearly plenty of people aren't OK. We are simply attempting to break the circle of hatred spawning more hatred.

Stage Five

In the final stage of the meditation we really let ourselves go. We try to apply whatever feelings of metta we have unearthed to all manner of other people, wherever they may be – or, indeed, to all manner of living beings, human and non-human. First of all we bring together the four people we have already included in the meditation, with the thought 'May I feel equal metta for all these people.' This means 'May I feel equally *strong* metta towards all four people.'

This doesn't mean that we stop having particular friends. It doesn't mean that we stop enjoying the company of some people more than that of others. It's just that when we awaken the faculty of metta within us we find that it's impartial. It's not that it's impersonal, but it goes beyond our personal view of things. It is a response deep within us that is activated by any living being. Almost all of us have it anyway to some degree; at our best we respond naturally to the life in others that we find in ourselves.

So in this stage we are developing the element of non-exclusivity in our metta. We imaginatively expand the range of our metta, gradually taking in all beings; wishing all beings well, wishing all beings freedom from suffering, wishing that all beings may make progress towards true happiness.

You can do this geographically, starting perhaps with those sharing the building you are meditating in, then taking in those living in that street, the locality, the town, the country, the continent, and so on. Or you might do it by first thinking of your friends, then your family, then your acquaintances, and so on. Or you might find another way of expanding outwards.

What is important is that we take in as wide a circle of people as we can. Sometimes this strikes people as rather abstract; we may wonder how we can really extend metta to people we have never met.

But if we let go of the limitations we impose on our imagination, we may well find this to be a very powerful experience.

I once saw a short documentary consisting of a number of interviews with people – from many different countries – who have travelled into space. What was remarkable about the film were the similarities in the responses of most of the people interviewed. Nearly all of them said how deeply affected they had been by the experience of seeing the Earth from space. They described in their own ways what might be called an experience of universal metta. Seeing how beautiful and fragile the Earth appeared when seen from space brought forth in these people, some of whom were pretty tough cookies, an overwhelming feeling of love, a feeling of wanting to take care of the Earth, a realization of just how precious life is. Sometimes when I do the Metta Bhavana I imagine what the Earth must look like from so far away.

Approaches to Cultivating Metta

I have said that one way to encourage and sustain a sense of metta in meditation is to use words. This means finding a simple phrase such as 'May I care for myself,' and using this phrase to stimulate a feeling. It does not mean that you sit and repeat in a dull and unreflective way – 'May I care for myself – may I care for myself.' We are not attempting a form of self-hypnosis.

If you are going to use a simple phrase to help you develop metta, you will have to give it some weight and feeling. You will also have to give it time to affect you. It's as though you take this idea in the form of words and drop it into your heart. You can actually imagine these words going down from your head into your body, coming to rest in your heart, or lower down still. And you can imagine these words setting up a sympathetic vibration in your body which is the feeling of metta.

If you want words to provoke an experience of metta they must be said with the intention to realize metta. That is the point of them. They suggest an emotional response, so they have to be said with feeling. If you happen to be a lawyer, no doubt you will see that this is rather a circular argument: it is as though we have to have metta in order to say the words with metta in order to produce metta. In a way this is true, but it is also true that there is no absolute division between thoughts, in the sense of words, on the one hand and feelings on the other. If you are sensitive to your words you will find that they always have an emotional component to them. There is no such thing as a completely abstract thought, free from all emotion. Even in the abstract field of pure mathematics, one of the qualities the mathematician looks for, or responds to, in an equation, is its elegance.

For some people words do not work very well in meditation. Even when they try to put warmth into them, the words still come out rather mechanical. If this is your experience after trying the practice a few times, don't just keep plugging away; try a different approach. For example, it might be that a simple image will work to stimulate a feeling of metta – a flower, say, slowly opening in your heart.

Alternatively, you could try using your memory. Remember a time when you were happy, and use this memory to reconnect with your feeling at that time. This can be of great help in the second stage: remember a time when you were in the company of a friend, having a good time or feeling a particularly deep connection with them.

It is also quite possible to base the metta practice in actual physical sensations. Let's say that, during the body meditation, you find yourself relaxing – well, you can encourage this sensation, allowing it to spread and grow. Just being aware of a sense of warmth and life in your hands can be the basis for encouraging metta to arise.

So there are many ways to approach this practice, and you should feel free to experiment. One word of caution: keep it simple. Complications can give rise to distractions – you will drift off into associated ideas or images and lose your basic intention, which is simply the cultivation of loving-kindness.

Now we'll do a led practice so that you get some idea about at least one possible approach to the Metta Bhavana: the development of universal loving-kindness.

The Metta Bhavana: *a led practice*

Before you start, think of three people you are going to use in the second, third, and fourth stages, so you do not spend the whole time picking and choosing people. Also remember to find a time when you will not be interrupted, and a quiet comfortable place to sit. Read through the practice a couple of times. You don't have to stick to it word for word – just try to get a good sense of it, or have a friend read it out loud.

Begin by taking the time you need to settle into your meditation posture. When you are comfortable, allow your eyes to close. As you close them try to let your face relax. Have a sense of not needing an expression on the face to set against the world or against your own experience – so that there is a feeling of the face being soft and open. If it still feels hard, introduce the ghost of a smile, which will encourage the facial muscles to relax. Try to allow your eyes to become still. You can think of them as soft and round, just resting.

Then take your attention down to your contact with the floor. Have a sense of the ground underneath you, supporting you. Try to let go of the weight of your body, giving it to the ground to support. Begin slowly to experience your body from the ground up.

Imagine your awareness filling your body, perhaps like a warm soft light – penetrating gently into your bones and muscles, relaxing the body as it moves upwards ... taking in the feet and the legs ... up into the pelvic area ... and into the lower back.

Be aware how your body responds to your directed attention, making that attention warm. The practice of loving-kindness begins by addressing ourselves with an attitude of loving-kindness. Take the time you need to contact your physical experience. Do not force your awareness into areas of the body that feel resistant to it, but be aware of that resistance, allowing the surrounding areas to soften and relax.

Draw your attention through your back, across your shoulders, and down your arms into your hands. For a few moments focus your attention on your hands. Check that they are relaxed and that your arms feel comfortable. Bring your attention back up your arms into your neck and up to the base of your skull.

Feel the muscles of your neck release and soften, and have a sense of your head being balanced rather than held. Become aware of the back of your head and then the top of your head. Feel the shape of your skull and allow the scalp to soften. Now return to your face, letting the whole of your face relax a little more ... the brow, the cheeks, the mouth, the jaw.

Feel the air against the skin of your face and become aware of your breath entering and leaving the body, finding space inside your body. Allow the breath to be easy and natural. Become aware of your body responding to the breath. Have a sense of your body being alive with the breath.

See if you can feel the movement of your body as the breath comes and goes. Find the movement low down in your belly, allowing the breath to soften the belly from the inside; then in your chest, feeling the whole of the rib-cage gently expanding to accommodate your breath, both at the front and the sides and the back.

Keeping an overall sense of stillness in your body, experience the soft rhythm set up by the breath. As you breathe in, have a sense of your chest opening, your shoulders relaxing. As you breathe out, let go into the breath, expelling any tension that you feel.

Slowly use the breath to help you begin to gather your awareness in your chest, inside your body where you imagine your heart to be. Imagine the breath is creating a connection between your head and your heart. Imagine the in-breath taking awareness down into the area of your heart and the out-breath allowing the feelings of your heart up into awareness.

Just spend a few minutes experiencing the breath as connecting up the head and the heart. Allow the breath to create a sense of spaciousness around your heart area. Allow yourself to experience what you feel, allow your heart to express itself into the space your breath is creating.

Then begin to imagine that the breath is carrying down into your heart a sense of well-wishing towards yourself. This may be a few simple words: 'May I care for myself,' or just your name spoken in your mind with warmth, or it may just be a sense of kindness. Keep it simple, just the intention of well-wishing directed down into your heart, into your body.

Give the words or intention time to settle, Don't rush or push yourself. Give yourself all the time in the world. 'May I be well, may I be happy.' Allow the heart to respond in its own time. Slowly experience your heart space filling with this simple idea. Continue in this way for a few minutes.

Now bring to mind a good friend. Invoke them, or evoke them, in whatever way works for you: with an image of their face, or by remembering their voice, or by remembering the last time you met. Bring them into your awareness.

Experience the warmth in your heart naturally turning towards them. 'May they be happy – may their life be how they would like it to be.' Take your time – not forcing out a feeling, just working with a clear intention to wish them well.

Allow time to experience any response you might have to this intention. Enjoy any positive feelings or thoughts that this intention generates towards your friend. Renew this intention whenever it feels it has been lost, and just keep the friend in mind.

Keep the practice simple: on the one hand maintain a sense of your friend, on the other develop a simple intention of well-wishing, of loving-kindness, together with an overall awareness of yourself. Continue this for a few minutes.

Allowing your friend to fade away from your attention, bring to mind the neutral person – who like yourself and your friend also wishes to be happy. Try to maintain the same kind intention, the same well-wishing as before, and simply extend it to include this person.

Keep your sense of them as bright and clear as you can, coming back to them if you find your mind moving away. Very gently, look beyond the limited view you have of this person. For once, don't just dismiss them from your mind once you have labelled them. If you like, use your imagination to evoke the individual richness and significance of their life.

May they be well, may they be happy. Don't force anything. Just allow whatever positive feelings you have to reach out to this person. Be sensitive to what is there, rather than trying to create some big feeling. Continue this for a few minutes.

Allowing the neutral person to fade out, bring to mind an enemy. Keep the face relaxed and open. Notice if the body has reacted to the introduction of this person. If you feel yourself tensing in your shoulders or your belly, take a few slightly deeper breaths, and soften your body.

Notice what your mind is doing. Has it got an old story it wants to replay about this person? Try to catch it before it goes off in this way; bring it back to the present and the intention to wish this person well.

Imagine this person well and happy, imagine them relaxed and joyful. See the other side of this person – from the side you find difficult. Try wishing this person well. Say their name and wish them well: 'May they be happy, may they be well.'

Give yourself time to see what that feels like to you. Allow yourself to feel what is happening in your heart; feel your resistance – or feel that you are letting go of old destructive patterns. Imagine what it would be like to let this person be, to wish them well in their life, to lay aside the negative feelings you keep hold of. May they be well. Continue this for a few minutes.

Now bring to mind all four people you have thought of in the meditation: the difficult person, the neutral person, the friend, and yourself. Imagine all of you together, imagine a feeling of metta between you. All of you recognizing one another's desire to be happy and wishing one another well.

Look for a positive response to all four that is the same, that is equal – the same deep response of solidarity with another human being. Now you can begin gently to extend this feeling of well-wishing outwards.

Allow your awareness to move outwards, an awareness imbued with metta. Slowly take in the street, the locality, the district, and so on … just moving outwards. Metta has a natural tendency to expand.

Wish all beings well as they are encountered in your imagination. You can think of all kinds of people, from all kinds of cultures. Try to imagine the tenor of their lives, and identify particularly the aspects we all have in common in some form or another. Again, you may want to listen to their voices in your imagination rather than rely on visual imagination.

Think not only of people you may naturally feel sympathetic towards, but also of the kinds of people towards whom you feel less sympathetic. Include bad people as well as good, criminals as well as victims, people you disapprove of as well as people who are OK. May all beings whatsoever be well, may all beings be happy, may all beings be free from suffering, and may all beings make progress. Continue in this way for a few minutes.

Now slowly bring the awareness back to yourself. Think: just as I wish all beings well, so too may I be well, may I too be free from suffering and may I make progress. Finally, come back to your body sitting on the floor, back to the breath coming and going, back to a sense of the room around you. Then slowly bring the practice to a close. Sit for a minute or two with how you are now feeling.

four

BIG MIND

The Metta Bhavana is a meditation that involves us in an imaginative expansion of the heart to include all that lives, all life. It involves us in the cultivation of what we could call 'big mind', which is a sense of expanded awareness that is free from selfishness at its centre. The development of metta is a slow process – it takes years rather than months – but from the very beginning of this process we feel the benefits.

We begin slowly to strip away the layer of dead feeling we have developed over the years that gives such a sense of isolation. We become more aware of the kindness that is part of the world, that is all around us on a simple day-to-day level. We begin to take just a little more time and care with others; we become slightly less prone to react with anger or frustration. We have introduced into our lives a means of keeping in the forefront of our awareness a desire to become more truly human, and a method by which to realize this desire.

In the end it is in our dealings with others, and in our day-to-day attitude towards ourselves, that we need to manifest metta. But by cultivating a clear intention to do so, through the practice of the Metta Bhavana, our patterns of negative feelings become much clearer.

We become more aware of the undermining inner voice, the over-critical remark. We become increasingly sensitive to the emotional tone of our existence, the emotionality that determines to such an extent the quality of our own existence and the quality of our contribution to the lives of others.

At first this can sometimes be a little disturbing. We become aware of just how many negative thoughts and feelings we have. We might think 'What an awful person I must be to think these things,' but that is only another form of self-hatred. We need to accept that all of us have built up, to various degrees, negative patterns. Now that we have a way of beginning to change them, we don't have to turn away from them or make out they are not there. On the other hand we don't want to wallow in them. They are part of the story, but only a part, and with the decision to move consciously towards the development of positive emotional states we can look forward to being less and less in the grip of such negative feelings.

It's not so much that we get rid of such states, but more that we see through them, so that they lose the power to move us; it's about 'naming the dragon'. Then, in a sense, they cease to be 'emotions', inasmuch as they no longer have the force to move us.

Even after many years of practice we may still feel, for example, some old feeling of jealousy rise up when we hear about the success of a colleague, but we will be very aware of what it is. We will not try to pretend it is not there, nor will we try to rationalize its existence. We will give it its proper name and then we will let it go. What we are learning to do is to be a lot more sensitive to what happens inside us — not sensitive in the sense of delicate, but robustly alert and alive to ourselves.

The Brahma-Viharas

To begin with it's probably best just to concentrate on the Metta Bhavana, the first of the *brahma-viharas*, rather than taking on the complete set. However, it is useful to have a general idea of the other three practices, since they highlight different aspects of metta, and bring into focus some of the pitfalls we might encounter.

Metta is the basic energy of well-wishing; it wants the best for all beings. But sometimes this energy can begin to get a little abstract; it becomes more of an idea, and loses touch with reality. We might have met people like this trying to sell us flowers at airports, or getting us to accept free gifts on the street. They have a beaming smile and a rather vacant look. Or else there are those people who are just too 'nice', and they want everything to be really 'nice' – which is of course really nice of them, but somehow it grates on us.

We might get a kind of clingy feeling about these people. They are very kind but we are a little uneasy; they and the situation seem a bit sticky. They are positive in a vacuous sort of way. We probably all know the feeling. We may even have some experience of laying the sticky stuff on a bit thick ourselves. There is a lot of it around. It seems to flourish in our culture. The commercialization of festivals like Mother's Day really brings it out of the woodwork – occasions when we are bombarded with misty-eyed sentimentality masquerading as positive emotion.

It is quite easy to mistake this sort of thing for metta, and this happens when our meditation practice has lost its sense of the real nature of life. Yes, we might wish people well, but the brute fact is that we all suffer, we are all unhappy sometimes. There is a lot of pain in the world, and in the lives of people we know.

The *brahma-vihara* that comes after the Metta Bhavana is called the *karuna bhavana*, the cultivation (*bhavana*) of compassion (*karuna*), and it directly addresses this suffering. It looks suffering straight in the face. In this practice we look upon the suffering of ourselves and others with metta.

When metta meets suffering, what arises is compassion – an active desire to do what we can to alleviate suffering. This is how the metta practice enables us to cultivate compassion. In turn, the cultivation of *karuna* helps us prevent our metta practice from getting too sweet and sugary.

The contemplation of suffering, however, can cause us to become rather despondent. There seems to be so much of it all around us, what can we effectively do to give help? If our sense of metta is not all that strong we might well fall into despair. This is where the next *brahma-vihara*, the *mudita bhavana*, or cultivation of sympathetic joy, comes in. We deliberately dwell on the positive side of life in order to counterbalance our sense of worldly suffering.

Mudita is the ability to feel joy at the good fortune of ourselves and others. We look upon our own and others' happiness and prosperity with metta. Seen as an aspect of metta, this is the response of metta when it encounters joy – whether in ourselves or in others.

It's a funny thing, but sometimes we tend to respond more cheerfully to other people's sorrows than we do to their joys. We can cluck around people making sympathetic noises if they are in trouble or having a difficult time, but if someone is really happy we can feel rather uncomfortable, even threatened. This tendency to have difficulty in responding positively to the achievements and pleasures of others is, of course, based in our tendency to compare ourselves to other people. It is as though someone else's joy takes something away from us, diminishes us in some way. This is a feature of our particular culture: we are taught that we can get anything we want – but not if someone else gets to it first.

However, we will find it a source of great joy to be able to rejoice in the good fortune and happiness of others, and we can consciously cultivate this ability by means of the *mudita bhavana*. It is certainly a vital aspect of metta.

The last of the four *brahma-viharas* is the cultivation of equanimity, which is known as the *upeksha bhavana*. It is a sort of combination of the other three. It is not a cold, detached, unemotional equanimity, but rather a warmth, a generosity, that combines with a realistic and balanced view of things. It sees things as they are, so when it is highly developed it is very close to insight. It sees the impermanence, the conditioned nature of all things; it sees that all beings are ultimately empty of self. At the same time it responds with compassion and joy to the suffering and prosperity of those same beings. It is not, however, overwhelmed by what it experiences.

In a sense, this brings us full circle, as the danger of trying to develop equanimity is that we become too detached. We may start to feel that we are above it all, when really we are just a bit alienated, a bit out of touch with the real world and cut off from our basic emotional warmth, our basic feelings of care and kindness, our basic solidarity with others. So we go back and start again with the practice of the Metta Bhavana.

I hope that is sufficient to give you some idea of these other practices. As I said, it is probably not appropriate to attempt them as separate practices if you are fairly new to meditation, because you need a firm foundation of metta in order to use the *brahma-viharas* effectively. You would also need the time to practise frequently for them to be beneficial.

But we can bear in mind that metta has these aspects to it. We can think of metta as a kind of light made up of these different colours – *karuna*, *mudita*, and *upeksha*. It is as though the white light of metta reveals these hues as it encounters the different aspects of the world. If we begin to feel a little out of touch with our practice of the Metta Bhavana it can be helpful to consider whether we might have become a little one-sided, a little too abstracted from the human experiences of joy and suffering.

The Metta Bhavana is a process of opening to the world, in all its aspects. We often think 'I can't do that, I'll get hurt. I have to guard against all the awful things out there.' The cultivation of metta gives us not only a more open heart but also a brave heart. In India it is said that when you walk through the jungle, you should, if possible, do so in the company of a holy man – someone who has replaced hatred with loving-kindness, in order to keep you safe from attack by wild animals. Where there is great metta there is no fear, and even wild beasts can sense love and fearlessness.

Inner Light, Outer Light

In Kenwood House on Hampstead Heath, one of the largest and most beautiful open spaces in London, there is a small art collection, including a Vermeer and a Rembrandt. These two works hang in the same room, which is otherwise quite spartan.

The Vermeer is a painting of a young woman playing a guitar. She is seated, and on the wall behind her hangs a painting of a landscape. This portrait has an almost photographic clarity about it, in that every detail is very distinct. As much care has been taken over the frame of the background painting as the rendering of the delicate hands of the girl in the foreground. It seems as though the ermine trim of the girl's jacket would feel warm and soft to the touch. The painting has a intimacy to it, enhanced by the direction of the girl's gaze. She looks to the right, towards a unseen person, perhaps her father or mother who has just entered the room to hear her playing.

On the opposite wall, and facing you as you enter, is a self-portrait of Rembrandt – executed late in his life. By this time his fame and fortune had waned. His life too is waning. The painting is quite dark. His robes and cap are rendered with large brush strokes, and the background is indistinct. The focus of the painting is this old face looking out at us, painted in great detail, with immense subtlety. The paint is heavily layered, giving the face the texture of age. The right eye in particular attracts the attention.

As soon as you enter the room it feels as though you are being drawn towards this old man who looks out at you from the dark canvas. You feel compelled to go and stand before him. You have the privilege of standing where Rembrandt would have stood while painting it. This image is of such power that you feel you are being seen by Rembrandt himself, suddenly alive once more. It is you he is looking at. It is sometimes hard to turn away from the old man's gaze. His look for me is the gaze of metta. It knows no place it will not go, and it goes everywhere with intense love. The absolute candour with which Rembrandt looks at himself is also compassion. His self-honesty and his compassion are two sides of the same thing.

When you do turn your back on him you get your first glimpse of the Vermeer. It is remarkable to me that such a contrast can harmonize so perfectly. They do more than complement each other, more than just set each other off; they play together, they seem to communicate. You feel happy that Rembrandt can feast his eyes on such a painting. Both seem to be essentially about light. There seems, in the Rembrandt, to be an inner light of self-knowledge, while Vermeer paints the girl and her surroundings with such detailed clarity that it radiates an outer light of objective knowledge. It is the same light directed inward and outward, both with a tremendous power.

The Vermeer creates a marvellous sense of space and clarity and equanimity, but also of care, almost tenderness. You trust the man who painted this. There is a quality of clarity and insight that you respond to. And you know that Rembrandt still has his eyes on you.

There you are in this room in the middle of London and you encounter these two paintings. While you have been there other people have come and gone. Some hardly notice these pictures, but in others you see a sense of recognition, and it is themselves that they recognize. The emotional content of these pictures finds some ground to express itself in those who see them.

The qualities we cultivate in meditation are there as our natural ground; they are there as our potential, almost as a bird is potential in an egg. An egg is not a bird — it is what it is, an egg — but it does have the potential to change completely. And we have the same sort of potential. Of course, an egg is transformed by biological forces, whilst we are transformed by the force of self-awareness. Biology will produce a bird, whilst self-awareness will produce an ever-present mindfulness and universal metta.

This quality of mind is not a quality of our own mind, strictly speaking. It is certainly dependent on the individual consciousness for its arising, but once arisen it goes beyond the individual. The idea is expressed with great elegance by Shunryu Suzuki when he talks about 'big mind' — the mind that knows no limits — as opposed to our own 'small mind', the mind that belongs to us and is caught up in ourself. Big mind can communicate with us through great works of art as well as through spiritual teachings. Big mind is cultivated not only directly, through meditation, but also indirectly, through the appreciation of art and nature and ourselves, as unique and universal expressions of life.

five

KEEPING MEDITATION ALIVE

We have already seen that meditation is not a matter of employing techniques in a robotic way. It is much more about taking a simple idea or intention and applying that idea in a clear and structured way. The structure of the meditation exists to help support our creativity, not to crush it. In this chapter I want to explore some simple ways of looking at our practice in order to help keep it as fresh and alive as the first time we meditated.

Intention

It is very important that we have a clear sense of intention, of direction: we should be clear about what we are aiming to do, i.e. to develop clarity and kindness. The single most important factor in our meditation practice is the desire, or intention, to cultivate mindfulness and metta. As long as that volition is there, it does not, in a way, matter too much if your meditation is not very concentrated. You will still find, over time, that it has an effect.

For example, if you start each day spending half an hour trying to develop metta, you will soon experience the effects of your efforts in your daily life. You may not feel a strong sense of metta during the meditation practice, but it will still affect the rest of your life. This is because you have at least cultivated an *intention* to cultivate metta. There is no need to worry too much about individual meditation sessions. Rather, you should encourage the attitude that you are cultivating within your meditation to spread out into the rest of your life.

However, cultivating a clear intention is very different from holding tight to an idea of how the practice should go. When we first take up meditation it is quite common to have what might be described as strong meditations. This can be due in part to what we call 'beginner's mind'. Beginner's mind is an openness to experience. It means taking a keen interest in the *process* of meditation rather than looking for *results*.

But after meditating for a while we may begin to have ideas about what we will experience. We feel frustrated if we don't achieve the same level of concentration as we did the day before. In fact, our experience in meditation is necessarily subjective – it depends on what we have got used to. Once we are used to a certain level of awareness, it will not feel the same as when we first achieved it. It can be a little like going to see a movie that has been over-hyped. Even if it's a good film, we feel let down because our expectations had been too high.

What happens in the case of meditation is that the same experience feels less of a big 'experience' once we are used to it. We have replaced an intention with an expectation – an expectation that we will experience something we have identified as a good experience. The more we bring to our practice in terms of expectations the more difficult it will be for us to stay with what is actually happening at the time. It is this ability to appreciate what is happening that we can call 'beginner's mind'.

One might expect the term 'beginner's mind' to refer to a rather immature attitude, but it is very important to try to retain or rediscover this faculty. If we are trying for a repeat of a past experience we will be disappointed. The real joy of meditation is that every time we sit to meditate we do not know what is going to happen. This is how a beginner feels naturally.

So we may slip easily into a pool of metta or we may be struggling just to keep awake. And we find it very hard not to grade these experiences as good, or bad, or indifferent. I like to say that there is no such thing as a bad meditation, unless it is one in which no *effort* is made. If we are distracted, but we make some effort to come back to the object of the practice, then that is a good meditation. We will only be able to make that effort if we have a sense of what it is we are trying to do – if we have an intention.

We have to be clear about the purpose of our practice, and at the same time keep a sense of openness to the actual experience of meditating. We are trying to cultivate a clear but flexible mind, a mind that knows where it is heading but is also able to enjoy the journey. This concept of intention or purpose is closely related to what we may call 'balanced effort'. You could say that balanced effort is the means by which we work with our basic intention of developing mindfulness and metta within a particular meditation practice.

Balanced Effort

The idea of effort is an important one in meditation. Meditation is a very active practice – we do not just follow the instructions and wait for it to happen. We actively engage with ourselves, with our consciousness. It is this ability to affect our state of mind that makes meditation possible. It is our self-reflective consciousness that we meditate with.

The whole of Buddhism is based upon the idea that, through our own efforts, we can change the way we are. Our emotional patterns, our ways of thinking and feeling about ourselves and the world, are not god-given or set in stone by our early childhood experiences. By the conscious application of awareness upon our mind, we can cultivate particular emotions and ways of being so that they begin to dominate our everyday experience.

The message of the Buddha was very clear. He was telling us that we had a real choice about the state of our own minds. What was needed was a clear intention to become more aware and loving, and the application of the effort necessary to become so – effort within meditation, above all.

However, the idea of effort in meditation perhaps needs to be understood differently from the way we normally understand effort. We cannot force ourselves to be different, nor can we passively rely on meditation techniques to change us. What is needed in our meditation is balanced effort, that is, the application of effort that is appropriate. We can identify two opposing tendencies that will clog the flow of our meditation – sometimes both in the same practice: laziness and wilfulness. Balanced effort involves counteracting these two tendencies whenever we become aware of them.

I remember a friend of mine teaching meditation, and he was saying, as meditation teachers do, 'If the mind wanders, bring it back.' Then he added, 'This does not mean bring it back like a police snatch squad bringing back an escaped felon.' What he was saying was that the effort we make should be infused with the quality we are trying to cultivate. We could say that effort isn't simply about quantity. It also has its own emotional tone, which needs to be congruent with the object of the practice. In other words, effort should be appropriate.

Some of us incline towards a hard, disciplinarian approach, trying to squeeze all the metta we can out of our reluctant hearts; and some of us are maybe rather too happy just to go with the flow, regardless of where the flow is taking us. It's a good idea to know which category we are in, as these tendencies point to unconscious attitudes that we probably bring to most things we do.

The idea of balanced effort, particularly in relation to the breath, is sometimes evoked by imagining that you are holding a small song-bird in your hand. If you hold it too tightly you will crush its delicate body, while if you hold it too loosely it will fly away.

This may all sound quite simple, but in fact it's not that easy, because it's not enough to think we know how we are. We need to be sensitive to our actual experience, rather than relying on ideas we have about ourselves. This is a rather interesting area, and one in which I have a pet theory. I think that very wilful people often think of themselves as lazy, and lazy people think of themselves as wilful.

It kind of makes sense if you think about it. If we think we are lazy, we will probably make a stronger effort to do things. But regardless of what we achieve, we will think it is not enough because we think we are lazy. So we will drive ourselves to do more. If, on the other hand, we think we are the kind of person who overworks, we will always be telling ourselves to take it easy. I am sure we have all met and perhaps worked with the kind of person who is always saying how much they do, but never seems really to get down to doing anything much at all.

Then there are people who seem able to get things done almost effortlessly. We had a cook at one of our retreat centres who was a joy to watch. He was often cooking for a hundred or more people, yet he seemed to have all the time in the world to do it. He was able to produce wonderful meals without breaking into a sweat. If you have tried cooking for that many people you will know how manic you can become over it.

Interestingly, cooks in Zen monasteries were chosen on the basis of their achievement in their meditation, as it was thought that the quality of energy used in the preparation of the food entered the food and affected those who ate it (a disturbing thought, perhaps, for those who frequent fast food outlets).

Well, whether or not you agree with my theory, it does seem to be the case that in meditation there is an appropriate level and quality of effort to be aimed at. Effort that is too hard or too soft, too little or too much, will tend to take us away from the object of attention. In the end all we can do is to try using more effort or less effort and see what happens. We will soon become sensitive to the various qualities of effort we can employ, and get a sense of balancing the effort within our practice.

Just don't assume that you already know. Try it out. When you sense that the object of meditation is slipping away, see if you can step up the amount of effort you are using and bring the object back into focus. If this stepping up of effort has the effect of making it harder to stay with the object, try relaxing the effort you are making. It really is a matter of feel – which you will have to develop through trial and error. However, we can perhaps get a better sense of this idea of balance by looking in more detail at the elements of ourselves that are involved in the practice of meditation.

BALANCING ENERGY IN MEDITATION

Another approach to the idea of balance in meditation is by way of a simple model of our experience that divides it into three broad areas – thoughts, emotions, and the body. While in the higher reaches of meditation there is a kind of fusing of these areas into a single experience of awareness, we can in general talk about them as to some extent separate areas of our experience.

To put it simply, we can say that these three areas need to come together in our awareness to create the feeling of completeness and integration that will deepen our meditation. In a sense, the practices themselves encourage this process of integrating head, heart, and body. But there will be times when our meditation will feel rather flat, dry, or one-sided – lacking in colour – even though we may be closely attentive to the object. If this is your experience it would be worth checking to see if you are perhaps over-investing in your purely mental experience, counting the breaths as though you were counting sheep. Then perhaps you would need to reconnect with the emotional richness – your enjoyment – of the breath, and feel the breath in the body like you feel the wind in your face when you walk by the ocean.

This is a very simple model to bear in mind: these three factors all need to be present in order for our experience to feel satisfying. We have already seen the importance of the body and the emotions as far as meditation is concerned, and we will go on to look at them briefly with regard to this idea of balance. But first we shall look in some detail at the area of thoughts, or mental activity.

Thoughts

Thoughts sometimes get a bad rap when it comes to meditation. Many people have the idea that meditation is something to do with getting away from thinking. Certainly it is true that we are trying to get away from what often passes for thinking – which is in reality little more than mental static due to over-stimulation. But thought that is clear and directed plays a very important role in the art of meditation.

I wonder if the 'heart' of meditation is in certain circles now over-emphasized. Sometimes it seems that we are at risk of falling into a kind of sentimental slushy 'spirituality'. People often seem to think that the spiritual somehow opposes the rational. But this is not true. It would be true to say that we are aiming with our practice to go beyond the strictly rational, but we are aiming to go beyond the strictly emotional and the strictly physical too.

Words like 'insight' and 'Enlightenment' obviously imply a sense of mental clarity. Clear and directed thought is an essential tool in helping us to become focused. It does have its limits, but very few of us have reached them.

We employ two main types of thought in meditation, sometimes referred to as 'initial thought' and 'sustained thought'. In fact they are both just thought, the difference being that one is a simple thought that stands alone, while the other is a directed line of thinking, or contemplation of a mental object.

Initial Thought

This is a simple 'idea' used to help us come back to the object and/or purpose of the meditation. It may be a single word or a short phrase you bring to mind – like telling yourself to wake up if you start to feel sleepy. But it needn't be a word at all. It could be an image – imagining a bright light, say, to wake you up.

In the Metta Bhavana we might use initial thought a good deal to stimulate metta. We might use a single word such as 'care', 'kindness', 'love', or a short phrase like 'may I be happy'. Sometimes I will get people just to say their name to themselves as a way of coming back to their actual experience. There are countless ways we can use this type of thinking, particularly in the early stages of trying to become a little more focused and to correct any tendency to drift off after we have gained a certain degree of concentration.

Here is a simple exercise to show how a thought can be dropped into your awareness. Sitting in meditation posture, imagine that your body is like a deep well, and that you are dropping a white pebble down into the well. After it hits the water, it spirals down deeper and deeper into the well and at some point comes to rest at the bottom. Now imagine that the pebble at the bottom of the well is subtly vibrating, and that these vibrations set up movements in the water.

In this way we can get a sense that we are able to affect ourselves on quite a deep level by using a simple thought or image. Once we have the general idea it is easy to substitute for the pebble whatever it is we want to resonate with, or we could just associate the ideas – perhaps by writing on the pebble.

I have described this exercise not because I think you need to do it, unless it happens to appeal to you particularly, but in order to convey the idea that when we use thought in meditation we need to give it some weight. We can drop ideas into ourselves and give them time to resonate within us. We need to allow ourselves time to respond to our directed thought.

Unless we give the idea some space and energy it will not really have much chance of doing what we want it to. In the Metta Bhavana practice, there is no point in repeating the words 'may I be happy' like a parrot, or like a record needle stuck in a groove. We should try to feel the meaning of the words. This means using what I would call the imagination – not in the sense that we are trying to make something up, but in the sense that we are trying to imbue an idea with meaning.

Notice in what tone of voice you say things to yourself. Words serve to express feelings, and they do this not only in an abstract way – in terms of literal meaning – but by tone and intonation and by intention. Our primary relationship with language is not with its literal meaning, but rather with its emotional texture. As young children we were sensitive to this emotional texture long before we had begun to master the actual meaning of words.

If we say to ourselves 'may I care for myself' in an off-hand way, we cannot really expect much to happen. But the same words imbued with imagination, with emotional colour, may well produce the resonance within us that we are looking for.

Sitting with your eyes closed, try saying your name to yourself. Notice how you say it. Try to say it with tenderness, with care. Give yourself time to feel any effect this might have. Imagine it going down into your body, filling your body. Try doing the first stage of the Metta Bhavana just using your own name, calling yourself back to yourself.

Sustained Thought

In meditation this means following a connected line of thought with a definite purpose in mind. We employ this kind of thought when we guide ourselves through our physical experience, as in a body meditation. We use it in the Metta Bhavana when, for example, we recall the qualities of our friend to stimulate our appreciation of them.

It is normal to find oneself quite concentrated when one leads a meditation, when one guides a class through a practice. This is the power of sustained thought at work. Later, we will see how we can use this sustained thought to help us overcome some of the distractions that crop up in our practice.

Mental activity cannot just be shut off in meditation. The mind has to be given something useful to get on with, otherwise it will just run off and fool around. In this way our minds really are rather like young children. There is a lot of energy there, and if this mental energy isn't engaged, it will tend to find rather irritating outlets. I often use the word 'fascination' when I teach the mindfulness practice. Just as children need to be entranced, fascinated, in order to engage their attention, so we need to become fascinated with the breath.

So the main point here is not to regard thought as a negative thing to be got rid of, but to learn to use it to help us go more deeply into the practice. Thought is the tool that is most readily available to many of us, and unless we employ it we will not get very far at all. At least to begin with, it is always going to be occupying our attention in one way or another. In fact, it is now known that during meditation blood flow to the brain increases significantly, making it more energetic, not less – so we may as well make the best of it.

In order to move into a more concentrated state we will have to use one or both of these modes of thinking. They contrast sharply with the usual way the mind works. If we close our eyes and attend to what is going on in us mentally, we will probably find, once we settle down, that thoughts just pop up and develop further thoughts in a sort of associative or discursive process. We think of one thing and by association this brings another thing to mind, and another, until before very long we find that we have moved a long, long way from the first thought, if indeed we can remember it at all. This kind of mental activity is largely devoid of self-reflective awareness – that is, devoid of the type of awareness we are cultivating in meditation. It is as though *we* are not deliberately thinking at all, but thoughts are somehow spawning further thoughts without our having any say in the matter. Our thoughts are mental orphans, unplanned and left to roam around with no meaningful future.

The real begetters of our thoughts are not ourselves but the constant streams of information we expose ourselves to. Our attention is pulled from one thing to the next, our heads are bursting with thoughts jostling to get a hearing, and in the general internal hubbub we never really pick up a clear message. The quality of the thoughts is not the issue here – many of them may be great thoughts – but if we give them no space we will never make anything of them. For example, a lot of people read 'self help' books, one after another, hoping that at least some of this wisdom is going to stick. And they are mystified when it doesn't. But if we stuff too much into the mind, we won't be able to digest anything. And when the appetite goes, we lose the flavour of what we are taking in.

When it is over-stimulated, the mind is eager to exhaust itself, thinking, thinking, thinking. It doesn't really care what it thinks. It is an addict for thoughts. And we might have taken up meditation because we are sick to death of this constant, restless, pointless mental activity. We want a little peace of mind.

But this kind of mind is like a child. We cannot just put it in the corner and expect it to sit quietly. We have to give it something to do, something it will enjoy. Eventually we will find that it begins to settle down. With patience we can learn to keep the mind occupied with a simple and enjoyable train of thought. And we will find that the calmer the mind becomes, the more subtle the thoughts become.

So we need to think in order to meditate. We need to cultivate clear, directed thought that is related to the practice we are doing. Of course this will also spill out into the rest of our lives. We will find that we are better able to apply our minds to things. We will experience our thinking as brighter and more focused. Thinking of this kind also has a positive emotional quality. We will find that clear, bright thinking is in itself an enjoyable experience.

Before we move on, it is worth mentioning one other kind of thinking that plays an important part in meditation.

Intuition

I like to think of intuition as simply a subtler level of thought and imagination. It is the ability to encourage the mind in a certain direction with a particularly light and subtle touch. I do not think intuition is a gift you are born with, but acquired through developing some degree of calm clarity. It is by the deliberate exercise of directed sustained thought or clear initial thought that we slowly build up the ability to use our minds intuitively.

At a certain point we find that the directions we are giving ourselves no longer always need to be made so explicit. As it becomes more concentrated, the mind becomes increasingly sensitive. If we know someone very well we might sometimes have the experience of being able to sense what they are feeling. Because we are 'in tune' with them we are able to respond to very subtle signals. This is a little like what happens when we are used to thinking in a directed way during meditation and we begin to become more deeply absorbed in the object of our meditation. To introduce a great clunking thought at this point, however well-meaning it may be, can actually jolt us off track if its quality of energy is in conflict with our mental state. It's like trying to push a shopping trolley; it never quite seems to go where you want it to unless you have a very light touch.

I don't know if homoeopathic medicine works on quite the same principle, but it's interesting that the more dilute a homoeopathic remedy is, the more effective it tends to be. Many of the remedies are diluted to such an extent that they have no chemically analysable active properties left in them at all. Nevertheless they evidently work, even on animals. Faint or subtle does not necessarily mean weak. And the imperceptible is not necessarily ineffective.

So what we could call intuition is a very useful tool in meditation. However, it does need to be based upon experience and developed over time. People often claim to be using this faculty when they are just being lazy. Free association, drifting from one thing to the next, seeing what happens, is not intuition. Intuition is the exercise of a very finely-tuned sense which has developed through *conscious* effort. If we wish to use this faculty we will have first to become experienced in using the mind in a clear, directed way. After a while, this ability will simply become a natural – though learned – response, and will no longer need to be operated in a heavy-handedly deliberate way.

When to Let Go of the Object of Concentration

We have seen that even – or particularly – in the development of intuition, we need to bring quite a degree of discipline to employing our thinking faculties. There is, however, a time and a place to let go of the object of concentration to some degree and allow the mind to move away from what we have set out to focus on. I say this a little reluctantly, because it is all too easy to get caught up in distractions that seem important at the time, but in fact have no real value.

But it would also be a mistake to stick slavishly with the object of concentration, absolutely regardless of what the mind may throw up. Meditation is a slow process of integrating disparate parts of our psyche; now and then some lost treasure will suddenly be unearthed, which is worth having a look at. The problem is that it is all too easy to mistake pieces of junk for treasure. Our mind in this respect is very cunning and will always be offering us alluring distractions.

It's like dreaming. There are some people who seem to think that you always want to hear about their dreams, that all their dreams are of great value and significance. They aren't, of course, although there are such things as 'big' dreams. Big dreams have a certain quality that distinguishes them from normal dreams: they feel weighty. It is not so much the content but the texture of them. The same sort of thing can occasionally happen in meditation, and like the big dream it is worth attending to.

For example, say you have no real memories before the age of seven and suddenly there pops into your mind a vivid image of yourself aged five. What should you do? Call it a distraction and return to the breath? I think that sometimes you just have to go with such things, see where they lead. However, it is the concentrated state of mind that has given rise to this experience, so if you let go of the meditation completely you will probably lose the treasure as well. It is therefore more a matter of allowing the former object of concentration – the breath, or the metta – to remain as a background to the new experience. This is quite different from just day-dreaming. It is like a big dream, so it should be listened to, but at the same time we should retain some connection with the practice. And this is not easy.

On the whole, we should not be drawn away from the object of the practice down interesting-looking by-ways. It's best not to think about important experiences in meditation until they turn up, which by their very nature isn't very often at all. People who have 'important experiences' probably also enthral their friends every day with full details of all their 'big dreams'.

Emotion

To outside observers Buddhism has in the past seemed to be a rather passionless business – an impression not helped by the fact that the term for the Buddhist goal, nirvana, is commonly translated 'extinction'. In fact, what we are working towards is not an unfeeling state, but rather what I would prefer to call a clarity of passion. We are trying to infuse passion with mindfulness, bringing together what we call the heart and mind into an integrated whole.

Meditation without emotion would be a dry affair, and it would not be able to engage our interest for very long. Emotions are – as the word itself suggests – what really move us. Without some degree of emotional engagement in the practices, there would be little sense of pleasure, and no real motivation to perform them.

However, while we can to some degree choose to think about something, it is far harder to make ourselves feel something. Emotions are going on all the time at some level of our being, and their very nature – as the word emotion suggests quite literally – is to move out, which is when we can become aware of them. If we do not let them move out, if we do not allow them to manifest even in our own minds, if we don't acknowledge their existence, then they find increasingly negative means of making themselves known.

An extreme example of this is the manifestation of certain physical illnesses that have as one of their causes the repression of emotion. Research has shown that men who suffer heart attacks relatively early in life are often those who had an inability to experience and express their feelings. It is as though the heart is no longer able to hold all the unexpressed emotion, and in the end it bursts.

We have already dealt with certain aspects of the process of using the body and using thought to contact feelings and emotions, but I want to say a little more, as this is a very important area. Buddhism draws a clear distinction between the terms 'feeling' and 'emotion'. 'Feeling' has quite a narrow range of reference: it means the simple reaction of pleasure or aversion to our experience of bodily sensation. Emotions, on the other hand, are more complex sets of responses that arise due to feelings interacting with our total being. In this sense, feelings are physiologically based, while emotions are more subject to our psychological conditioning.

Clearly, feelings based on physical sensations have a strong effect on our emotional state. Pleasure tends to make us happy, whereas pain or discomfort tends to make us unhappy. The same is true on a mental level. If we are under stress, through feeling either overloaded or under-employed, we will be unhappy, while if we are engaged in an interesting project we will be happier and more energetic.

So much, so obvious. However, we can use this connection between feelings and emotions in meditation. To begin with, we set up the body in a comfortable manner, and encourage a sensitivity to the sensations within it, particularly pleasant sensations. These may be no more than feelings of stillness or relaxation, but they should be dwelt upon, because taking this sort of interest in our physical sensations feeds into our emotional state.

We can also use the imagination to bring out what is enjoyable in our sensations. Take, for example, the simple sensation of the breath gently opening up the chest, the rib-cage slowly expanding with the incoming breath and then relaxing with the out-breath. If we add to this sensation the idea of the body opening to life as we breathe in, and a sense of giving ourselves fully to that life as we breathe out, we will find that the thought strengthens the sensation, and the sensation supports the thought. We can set up a kind of positive feedback between the two.

Together they will encourage an emotional response in us which will in turn deepen the whole of our experience of the breath, allowing our mind to become increasingly absorbed in the practice. The first stage of the metta practice can be carried out more or less entirely on this level of paying notice to the body, and encouraging through the imagination an enjoyment of ourselves as a physical experience, an enjoyment of our physical self.

We can, for example, bring our attention into the area around our heart and allow the breath to open up this area, while imagining a warmth or a soft light slowly developing inside our chest and then spreading throughout our body. This is very likely to give rise to a positive emotional response towards ourselves. We are in fact wishing ourselves well – we are just using a rather different approach to the stimulation of metta.

Another way of encouraging our emotions to be part of our meditation experience is through the use of thought in a more direct manner. We might bring to mind some idea or memory that holds an emotional resonance for us. Personally, I sometimes read a poem before I meditate, one that I know well, and that I know will tend to encourage emotional sensitivity.

I always take a few poetry books with me on retreat. Not only do I find that certain poetry helps me to a direct contact with my emotions, I also find that the awareness I build up when meditating a lot allows me to deepen my understanding and appreciation of poetry. In time, it seems to me that certain poems can become positively charged – reading them is a little like plugging oneself into an 'emotion battery'. I am sure the same is true for the visual arts and music.

Traditionally, Buddhist meditation practice takes place within a context dedicated and designed to support and encourage the development of awareness and kindness. And that context includes a strong aesthetic element. Beautiful pictures adorn the walls, there is chanting of devotional verses, and of course an image of the Buddha on the shrine, radiating calm and compassion, is the focal point. And there is a purpose to it all, which is to include our emotions in our practice.

Sometimes when we meditate it will seem that while we have plenty of emotional energy, it is of a rather different kind to that which we think of as positive. It certainly isn't unusual to find that if we try to stimulate a feeling of metta towards ourselves, what in fact happens is that another seemingly contrary emotion arises. It seems that we often have to work through a layer of other emotions before we begin to get in touch with metta.

Sadness and anger, in particular, come to the surface. I do not see such emotions as contradictory to the development of loving-kindness. Some of us invest a lot of energy in keeping such emotions at arm's length, when in fact they are very much part of the human condition. All of us suffer from feelings of loneliness and isolation – they seem to be part of the price we pay for possessing self-reflective awareness. On one level we are always alone, and we can never be fully otherwise except through a fundamental shift in the way we perceive ourselves in relation to the rest of reality.

However, we tend to think that emotions such as sadness and anger are bad, even perhaps shameful, and we do what we can to avoid experiencing them. In meditation we are creating a vessel, an overall context, in which such feelings can be experienced, and we should not be scared to allow them room. What we try to do is contain them in a context of mindfulness and metta. Meditation is not a way of avoiding such feelings or of constructing a perfect internal world, free of the more painful aspects of human life. Rather, it is about creating a space where feelings find room to be experienced without the harmful effects they might have under other circumstances. Unexpressed feelings will find a way to be heard, and in order for them to do this we often have to construct destructive situations in the concrete world. The more conscious such feelings are, of course, the less we need to do this.

I have known people who have spent their first few months of metta practice in tears. It is as if finally they are able to feel the pain that has been no more than an unidentified sense of foreboding for so many years. They are by no means rare. Through meditating we are inviting our emotions into awareness. Although it can sometimes feel painful, it is also a great relief to be more fully aware of the fears and pains that inhabit our twilight consciousness. In the end they are just emotions. Their destructive power lies not in the clear experience of them but in the shadows where we cannot bring ourselves to shine the light of awareness.

In 'The Inn at Tamagawa Station' the Zen poet Ryokan expresses well the relationship between so-called positive and negative feelings. It seems we cannot blot out one without blotting out the other.

Midautumn – the wind and rain are now at their most melancholy.
A wanderer, my spirit is inseparable from this difficult road.
During the long night, dreams float from the pillow –
Awake suddenly, I have mistaken the sound of the river for the voice of the rain.

Meditation shows us that we do not have to avoid our emotions, that they do not control us, that they come and go – if they are acknowledged. Even the most terrible feelings of hatred, while they certainly should not be encouraged or unduly dwelt upon, are still part of our meditation experience. When they occur, it is important to try to experience them in the vessel of mindfulness, to give them room to be felt, to create a safe context for the experience of them. We will be taking a closer look at negative emotion and how to work with it in the next chapter.

I want to add a few words about sadness, as I believe this emotion is to some degree a positive one, at least on a relative level. One way of talking about the aim of Buddhist practice is to say that we are trying to come to terms with how things really are. Our suffering comes mainly from not fully accepting the fact of impermanence. According to Buddhism, impermanence is not just one particular quality of things, it is the defining quality of all things. There is only impermanence.

This might at first seem a negative view of the world, but it is not really a view at all. It is just the way things are. It is not a way of looking at things but the ineluctable nature of things themselves – including, of course, us. We resist this realization quite tenaciously, we want things to remain the same, we want something lasting. But beauty is of its essence born out of impermanence. A true experience of the real delight and joy that the world and relationships can afford us is based in the acceptance of their impermanence. And within this is a feeling of sadness. Sadness is the emotion we are trying to avoid in maintaining a view that denies the full significance of impermanence. This emotion of sadness needs to be felt. It will be present until we have taken on the fact of impermanence more fully.

It seems to me that the ability to appreciate ourselves, and others, and the world around us, is linked to a willingness to feel sadness: not a self-indulgent sentimental sadness but a sadness which is an expansion of the heart towards the world. It is this quality, it seems to me, that is to be found in Ryokan's poetry. There is a full acknowledgment of sadness and also a movement of the heart that goes beyond those feelings. The movement is from an individual perspective towards a more universal sense of how things really are.

It is when we acknowledge emotion that it becomes possible for us to transform it. As long as we deny our suffering we cannot work creatively with it. Through meditation we are trying to have a deeper, more authentic experience of ourselves. This does not mean that we magically move beyond suffering, but it does mean that we open up the possibility of doing so.

The Body

We have already dealt with the body in some detail, both in Chapter One and in relation to thoughts and emotions. As we saw in the body meditation, we try to ground our experience in the immediate and concrete, allowing the experience of our emotional and mental state to root itself in awareness of the body. Throughout our meditation the body gives us an experience to come back to whenever we feel we are losing our way. If we pay attention to the body in meditation it will help to keep us in our present experience. While the experience of the body may become increasingly subtle as we become more concentrated, it remains the foundation of our self-awareness.

There is no absolute division between thoughts, emotions, and physical sensations. Meditation is neither a mental activity, nor an emotional activity, nor a physical one. It is mental and physical experience fused together with emotion – or, rather, infused with emotion. Emotion is a sort of bridge between the body and the mind. Its origins may well be in simple bodily feeling but it will also directly affect our mental experience. In this way we are trying to integrate these separated aspects of ourselves into a unified experience. By maintaining an awareness of all three we can begin to appreciate their interrelationship; and as we become more concentrated we will also feel a sense of them gathering together around the object of concentration.

For example, in the Mindfulness of Breathing we try to establish a firm sense of the breath in the body. This physical awareness is supported by clear and directed thinking and also by an emotional receptivity to the experience of the breath. This is what full awareness means. If one of these elements is missing from our experience the meditation will have less depth; it will be less rich, less satisfying, less full.

So we are looking for a balanced sense of ourselves, a broad awareness of our experience, which will support and enrich our ability to appreciate the object of meditation. We will tend towards losing contact with at least one of these aspects of our experience, and when this happens we will find it increasingly difficult to remain with the object of concentration. If we feel we are losing the thread of the practice we need to check that the background of our practice contains an awareness of our body, emotions, and mental activity.

In the early stages of concentration we can work quite deliberately with these elements of awareness. As we become more concentrated a fusing of them will begin to occur, which will give rise to a sense of well-being and integration that will help us maintain that concentration.

seven

THE FIVE HINDRANCES

So far, we have been looking at the process of trying to produce and maintain positive mental states in quite general terms. We have seen that this is not a passive exercise but, rather, one in which we try to engage as consciously and fully as possible. We have established that we need to make an appropriate effort to maintain the object of our meditation as well as cultivate a broad background awareness that supports the awareness of that object.

Sometimes, however, we will find that these general approaches to our practice do not seem to be enough to stop our mind moving away from the object. And it may be that there is a dissenting element dominating our experience to such a degree that we do not really feel able to engage fully in the meditation. In this chapter we will be looking a little more closely at the kind of things that can inhibit the deepening of our meditation experience.

In meditation we withdraw our attention from the outside world, we move away from sense-based consciousness, and then see what happens, see what is there. The first step is to simplify our sense experience, reduce its input, and practise fully experiencing it – something we cannot do when it is passing through in a rush. So to begin with we need to bring our awareness to our present experience of ourselves, to those aspects we have just been considering – thoughts, emotions, physical feelings.

Normally, although our experience is dominated by what we are taking in through our senses, we give ourselves little time for all this sense experience to settle within us; sense experience is piled upon sense experience. Often this feels unsatisfactory, but instead of trying to simplify our experience we continue to seek out new sensations that we hope will do the trick. We want to believe that the world, in the sense of what is outside of us, can supply us with all the essential components for our contentment and happiness and assemble them too. We want to believe it is a matter of finding just the right job or the right sexual relationship for everything to fall into place.

Of course these things are important – we need to be nourished by friendship and satisfying external experiences; we need to feel that we are doing something of worth with our lives. Yet our ability to be nourished by the external world, to find enjoyment and fulfilment in the things that we do, is largely dependent on our internal mental states.

Our addiction to external experience is based in a sense of internal impoverishment, a kind of hunger and restlessness. If we don't see this, our experience becomes increasingly shallow, and the only way forward seems to be to seek out bigger experiences. Either that, or we give up. We become cynical and adopt an attitude of hard pragmatism, experiencing life as something to be got through.

If we really take the time to examine the underlying emotional tone of our lives we will find, I am afraid, that it is very largely dominated by negative emotions. It is this general tone of variously combined negative emotions that manifests as the constant need we have to be doing something – talking on the phone, watching television, eating, preferably all at the same time. We use this kind of half-experienced activity in order to keep our awareness on a shallow level where we won't feel the underlying pain or unsatisfactoriness of our lives.

In meditation we come to experience these tones of negative emotion as hindrances to our ability to access more positive states of mind. At the same time, we have the time and space to experience them more clearly and directly in this form, and therefore begin to dismantle them.

As long as these states of mind form the background to our experience it is very hard to enjoy what we do. They are not particular to meditation, nor are they a product of meditation. They just become more obvious to us when we try to meditate, because we have consciously put aside the ceaseless activity we use to inhibit our experience of them. So meditation is a great place to work with these mental habits. It is because we are consciously trying to develop positive emotional/mental states that the hindrances opposing them become highlighted.

If our meditation is going well, so that we are moving towards more positive states of mind, all we need to do is go with the practice. We don't need to look for problems, we don't need to hunt down our negativity like some dangerous animal. Sometimes, however, we will find that we do not seem able to move in the direction we wish, that our experience in meditation feels stuck.

At these times we need to make a creative and active intervention. The first thing we have to do is be clear about what is happening. We need to bring into awareness what is hindering our progress. The five hindrances are a traditional way of viewing our experience and bringing a sense of clarity to what is happening.

It is said that whatever is inhibiting the development of mindfulness and metta can be categorized as one or more of these five hindrances. They allude to the tone or quality of feeling of our experience, rather than the more conscious mental content. For example, we might be trying to meditate but we just cannot stop thinking about work. The hindrance is not the thoughts about work as such; it is the underlying emotional energy connected with – and giving rise to – the thoughts we are having. We might be worried about our work, or we might be excited about it, and it is this general quality of our thoughts that we need to identify and deal with. Rather than getting caught up in the particular details of our thoughts, we want to go deeper into the background emotional state that is giving rise to these details.

The five hindrances are (1) hatred or ill will, (2) desire for sense experience, (3) restlessness and anxiety, (4) sloth and torpor, and (5) doubt and indecision. Let's take a look at these in turn, and try to get a feeling for them. Then we will look at some general approaches to dealing with them.

Hatred or Ill Will

As I have already mentioned, hatred is regarded in Buddhism as a very strong attachment. When we have feelings of ill will we tend to hold on to them, to nurture them. We encourage minor irritations to mature into hateful feelings. They seem to fascinate us and can easily come to dominate our inner life. Sometimes they are directed towards external objects: other people – sometimes they turn inwards: we look for imperfections in ourselves and resent what we find.

We need to learn to unhook these feelings from their object. It is the object that we use to justify such feelings and keep them fed and thriving. Ill will can take many forms, of course. But in meditation we try to cut through this sort of thing. We are not concerned with the rationalization of such feelings – who said what to whom, or in what precise way we have been offended or slighted. Exploring all the details of our outrage simply serves to stop us really experiencing the emotional core of these feelings, which is harmful to our own well-being.

We have to be able to distinguish between ill will, or hatred, and anger. There is something stuck and inturned about ill will; we do not really want things to change for the better as this would remove the grounds for the feelings in which we have invested so much. Sometimes it is our refusal to experience our anger that leads to the more insidious and festering feelings of ill will. I am sure we have all had the experience of being direct about our feelings and clearing the air. The clean, honest expression of our feelings can cut through the rationalizations associated with ill will and lead to a resolution of a painful situation. However, there is a thin line between anger and ill will, and we need to be careful not to foster either of them. In the end it is probably best to try not to operate on the basis of either of these emotional states.

To begin to deal with such feelings in meditation we need to acknowledge them as honestly as possible. We have these sorts of feelings, and we have to take responsibility for them; we can't just say 'It's his fault I'm angry' – and wait for him to do something to restore our good humour. Our anger belongs to us, and it's up to us to do something about it. We know this really. There are times when no one seems to be able to disturb our good humour; and there are times when everyone seems to be more or less objectionable.

So first we have to realize that we are subject to ill will. If we have a strong investment in a certain idea of ourselves as, for example, a very 'reasonable' type of person, it might be quite hard for us to do this, as it challenges the idea we have of ourselves. It is not at all uncommon for people to find, at some point in their practice, that they experience a lot of anger, even rage. It is all that ill will built up over years of 'being a reasonable sort of guy' coming to the surface.

When this happens we need to acknowledge these feelings frankly and keep in touch with a desire to work through them. Strong feelings in meditation can be of great help. They contain a lot of emotional energy. We need that energy to be available to us in order to access some positive emotion. Indeed, in meditation it is possible for our emotional energy to flip over quite dramatically from negative to positive. For this to happen we need clarity and mindfulness. If the feeling is seen clearly and its damaging aspects are acknowledged, then it will tend to change.

We must not be afraid to feel in meditation. Meditation can be very empowering in the sense that we learn to experience ourselves more fully and honestly. By doing so within a context of clarity we also learn that these unacceptable feelings do not need to be feared; we do not need to be controlled by them.

This is a very important area. We do not have to look very far to observe the power of negative emotion, particularly unacknowledged negative emotion. History is full of horrendous acts of barbarity, dressed in notions of religious or national or racial purification – horrors which suggest to us that civilizations wish away negative emotion at their peril.

It is comforting to think that the people who perpetrate such horrors are somehow 'bad' and that we ordinary decent folk are 'good'. But while it may well be true that some people are more inclined to evil than others, it is dangerously naïve to think that we are free of the kind of emotional tendencies that could, under certain circumstances, lead us, perhaps gradually, to truly evil action. Buddhism does not address itself only to 'good' people. It observes that all of us are capable of violent hatred. But it also observes that by the same token we are capable of sublime compassion. The matter cannot be left to chance – the stakes are too high. We all need consciously to cultivate our impulses for the good and work towards the transformation of our negative aspects.

In order to take responsibility for ourselves we have to realize that we can and do actively create our own states of mind. It is true that a whole web of conditions have made us what we are, but we are still capable of self-conscious change – and we are responsible for this change.

Closely associated with hatred is fear, and again it is quite common for this emotion to surface at some point in our practice. Many of us have feelings of shame around our fear. It undermines the idea we have of ourselves and our world. People who survive disasters are known to be prone to long-term post-traumatic stress involving panic attacks, such is the devastating effect on the psyche of a sudden experience of intense fear.

We shouldn't try to force these feelings out in the open so that we can zap them with our love gun. But negative emotions do not thrive in a situation of clarity and metta. Meditation has its own organic process – it is self-regulating. Given time, honesty, and gentle persistence, these feelings will come into the light of awareness and by then we will be ready to deal with them. What meditation requires is a wish simply to see ourselves as we really are. Behind these forbidden feelings of fear and anger is a lot of pain and loneliness, but if we can uncover these a tremendous energy is there to be released in another direction – towards joy and compassion and loving-kindness.

Desire for Sense Experience

This is the most common of all the hindrances. In fact it is so everyday that we hardly notice it. For many of us that's what is happening in our minds most of the time. Sometimes it has to stop before we realize it was there in the first place. It includes all the kinds of day-dreaming with which we please or excite ourselves. Basically, it takes us away from a world in which we cannot always have what we want into an imaginary one, or a memory, where we can.

It tends to be closely allied to enjoyment through the senses, so it includes – obviously – sexual fantasies, food fantasies, etc. (the list is as endless as the human imagination). But it also includes the more subtle pleasures of just thinking about something: in Buddhist psychology the ordinary human mind is treated as one of the sense organs.

On the whole, these distractions tend to be rather facile. But they are nevertheless powerful, as they tap into habitual patterns of thought: deep, well-worn grooves. They are therefore rather hard to get out of. I remember someone on a retreat very honestly admitting that the first week of his meditation was more or less taken up with sex and windsurfing – and this was a fairly experienced meditator. (I didn't ask if he ever managed to combine the two without falling off.)

We will soon become acquainted with desire for sense experience. It is sometimes called 'monkey mind', from the image of a young monkey frolicking in a tree laden with fruit; he does not even bother to finish one fruit before he leaps to grasp the next. The hard part is to catch ourselves doing this kind of thing before we become lost in it. It is very different from the kind of thought that is useful in our practice, but we have somehow got to try to get the little monkey interested in the meditation. If we just lock him in a cage he will set up an awful howling.

Hindrances often overlay one another, and this sort of distraction is sometimes what we could call a 'presenting distraction'. That is, we encounter this hindrance partly just out of habit, or to occupy ourselves so as not to confront other feelings lurking a little deeper down.

This hindrance pairs up with ill will in so far as they are opposite sides of the same coin, one being based in craving and the other in aversion. They are both very strong tendencies within us, so we have to be realistic and expect them to turn up from time to time during our meditation practice.

Restlessness and Anxiety

Here is another faithful friend. This hindrance has two levels of manifestation. It may present itself in the body, so that we just cannot get comfortable, we cannot settle down, or we're distracted by awful itches. Alternatively, it may be more mental, in that we are worried about something. Did we turn all the lights off? Where did we put that vital piece of paper? If you tend to be a bit of a worrier, then you will tend to be a bit of a worrier in meditation as well. If you are, you will find that however secure and carefully controlled your life may be, your mind is always capable of coming up with something 'worth' worrying about.

People are often motivated to learn to meditate by this habit of mind. Clearly it also makes it quite hard to settle down to meditate, but it's effective as a motivator because, unlike the previous hindrance, it is not even slightly enjoyable, and it is noticeably abated by even a little practice of meditation.

The manifestations of this hindrance can, like those of the others, be seen in part as habits, ways of thinking that we have developed over the years. At one time they might well have served a useful function, but once they turn into habits and develop a life of their own, they not only become useless, but, like Frankenstein's monster, they turn against their creator, and become a haunting presence we can't shake off.

This particular hindrance seems also to be part of the spirit of our age, so it is quite likely that we function on the basis of this particular mental state most of the time. It might well be that both our work and leisure are driven by restlessness and anxiety. And because it is so pervasive we can, as with desire for sense experience, mistake some of its manifestations for rather positive qualities. Having 'drive', being 'high-powered', 'motivated', and so on, are desirable qualities. We may feel that if we discourage this kind of feverish energy we will lack the will-power to make it in the real world.

However, from the point of view of real life, we can transform this energy into something far more satisfying and effective. Of course, it might be that such a transformation will not only challenge our self-view, but also make us re-examine our values in relation to the world. But this does not mean that we will become passive and lazy; rather, the clarity and positive emotion that meditation promotes will help us to engage more fully and energetically with the world.

Sloth and Torpor

This is the converse of restlessness and anxiety, in that as soon as we begin to meditate we slip into a warm bath of unconsciousness. This too can be a hindrance that manifests mainly in the body or in the mind. Its physical manifestations are that your posture will tend to sag, your head will droop, and you may feel yourself tipping forward. As a hindrance this is quite different from just being worn out from a long day's work: we know this because as soon as we stop meditating we feel full of energy. As a mental hindrance, it ranges from a kind of fuzziness or dullness to somnolence or stupor. It can be a very frustrating visitor, and hard to shake off once it has got a hold, as by its very nature we lack the clarity and presence of mind to be aware of it.

If you tend to suffer from this hindrance you should make sure you do not contribute to it by meditating when you are tired or hot, or just after you've had a heavy meal. Although it is the opposite of the last hindrance you are liable to get regular visits from both, even in the same meditation. They are related, in that if we operate from the basis of restlessness it is not unlikely that we will sometimes also have periods of sloth.

In its most extreme form, this fluctuation from a restless state to one of sloth is similar to a manic-depressive cycle. From being over-stimulated and excited the mind is likely at some point to collapse into a numbed, exhausted state. Normally in meditation we are not dealing with this tendency in such an extreme form, but we will soon notice that we do have quite significant swings. Meditation is a real opportunity to see the mind in action, in a way that our everyday lives do not allow us the time or space to.

Doubt and Indecision

It is sometimes said that this is the main hindrance to meditation – not because it is the dominant one (or at least not in the sense that we are aware of it), but because it makes it difficult to deal with the others effectively. In this sense it often underpins our experience in a general way when we are distracted.

It is linked to not having a clear intention when we meditate, and lacking a sense of confidence that we can meditate at all. It is nothing to do with a rational scepticism about meditation. (There is, after all, no reason to believe something just because you find it in a book.)

Doubt as a hindrance is basically not very conscious. It has an undermining quality, often based in feelings of low self-worth.

To some degree we all experience this self-doubt; this might come as a shock to those who regard themselves as confident. It is, of course, not peculiar to meditation. As with all the hindrances it is a mental habit built up over many years. It underlies not only a lack of confidence but also a kind of bullish over-confidence. What we need to develop is a realistic sense of our own capacities which allows us to work with our own mental states in a creative way.

It is a sad fact that many people's lives are dominated by a cynicism about themselves and the world around them, a lack of belief in the possibility of positive change in themselves, and of purpose in life generally. In its extreme – but not uncommon – form it manifests as a nihilism that sees the world as meaningless, and human life as having no higher significance.

The reasons for this are complex. Today we hear a lot of talk about alienation, lack of values, the break down of traditional patterns of life, and so on. Buddhism does not offer easy answers to these issues. It simply addresses the individual directly; it says that you can yourself experience the benefits of cultivating positive emotions and mindfulness. It doesn't ask us to believe in something outside ourselves – some divine power or political theory – that will intervene to make everything OK. It suggests instead that we look more deeply at our own experience and address the condition of our own minds directly. It is through the real experience of being able to change ourselves that we develop confidence in the potential of human consciousness to transcend greed and hatred.

When we begin to feel the effects of our own efforts, we find ourselves opening to the possibility that life can improve, that there really is more to it than the mindless pursuit of power and wealth.

114

According to Buddhism it is only through individuals' efforts to develop that meaningful change can come about. This certainly doesn't mean that such change should not be supported by political and social action; but this action can only have a lasting positive effect if it is based in metta, awareness, and insight. Social policy based in greed or hatred or selfishness will only perpetuate these sad states of mind.

The Five Hindrances as Basic Emotional Tendencies

The list of the five hindrances gives us a way of categorizing our experience of distractions. It is an exhaustive list in that every state of mind that hinders our concentration can be traced to one of these five basic emotional patterns. The hindrances are not, of course, the same as what we usually think of as distractions – outside noise, physical discomfort, and so on. They describe not particular experiences or sensations, but rather the underlying emotional tone that conditions our response to those experiences and sensations.

The list of the five hindrances goes back at least to the Buddha's time – so it isn't just someone's neat idea, waiting to be replaced by another neat idea. It has been accepted for a very long time as representing accurately the basic patterns that human emotionality tends to take. These patterns do not arise from nowhere, but are being conditioned and strengthened all the time. It would be true to say that if we are not in an aware, positive state we are to some degree in the grip of one or more of these five negative mental attitudes.

While meditation gives us the opportunity to work directly on these states of mind, we also need to look at the conditions that are producing them. In itself, meditation is not enough to eradicate these mental states if the rest of our lives is encouraging and reinforcing them. The best way to explore the way the conditions under which we live affect our mental states is simply, in a sense, to remove those conditions. You just make a deliberate choice to spend a bit of time completely alone, to experience not 'having' to do anything. While the idea of being alone can seem quite frightening, it seems to me that if we never try it we are missing out on a whole dimension of what it is to be human.

We live in a culture in which many of us feel loneliness without ever being truly alone for more than a few hours. Our ability to enjoy others and to appreciate their company is dependent on being able really to enjoy and appreciate our own company. Without some sense of emotional self-reliance we necessarily live in fear that the friendship of others might be withdrawn; and so to be able to value being alone forms the basis for an ability really to be with others.

Our interaction with others, our relationships, our friendships, are the most important things in our lives. Our lives would be totally empty without them. However, in relation to the hindrances, a life without occasional times of positive aloneness gives us no real chance to experience the hindrances in their basic form.

If we are constantly having to interact with others, we are also often having to cover up what we are feeling or to modify our response to things in order to get along. We might spend all day having to be pleasant and cheerful when underneath we are in a crabby mood; we then get home and explode at the kids or fall into a kind of lethargy, blobbing out in front of the television.

Often our emotional states are so difficult to handle because we do not get the time to experience them, free from the pressure of other people. While we are constantly busy and interacting with others it is all too easy to think of these hindrances as being produced by other people. Rather than just experiencing the fact that we feel restless, we will find something in the outside world to blame for this condition. If you are alone for a few days or weeks you begin to have to own these tendencies. When you get angry there is no one else to blame for it; it's just you, as it always is, but this time you know it.

During periods of solitary retreat you begin to experience the hindrances in a new way. This is because to some degree being alone breaks the chain of events that perpetuate these states. If you wake up in a bad mood and then have to go to work, no doubt the subway will be overcrowded, the bus will be late, and your boss will give you an impossible task: i.e. the world will conspire both to vindicate and to encourage your bad mood. On solitary retreat it is a lot easier just to see that it is you that are in a bad mood, and a lot harder to disassociate yourself from the internal situation.

I have also found that longer solitary retreats have to some degree changed the way I think of my own emotional life. Sometimes one can be in an emotional state that has the potential at least to be very creative, but the demands of normal life make it feel uncomfortable to be in that state. I believe that we no longer value solitude, often mistaking the normal human need to contact oneself more deeply in this way for depression.

If you feel a need to be quiet and reflective (in itself a positive need) everyday life often makes that need impossible to fulfil. People keep saying to you 'What's up with you? You're very quiet,' as though it's rather suspect not to be 'your usual self'. You end up feeling guilty, or you 'make an effort to cheer up'.

Our society has made it 'normal' to live frenetic, restless lives, lives packed with events and shopping. We are so used to living in such an anxious, wired state that if we stop feeling like that we start to think there's something wrong with us. It is our lives that give rise to our mental states; the five hindrances are the consequences of a life led in an unbalanced way.

Through meditation we can begin to experience the mental states that are the result of a deliberate effort to calm down and encourage positive emotional patterns, and we start to get a sense of what it would be like to live a life that promotes positive mental states.

eight

WORKING WITH THE HINDRANCES

Acknowledgment

The first thing to acknowledge is that these hindrances happen to all of us. We each have our particular favourites, but at some point we will experience them all. They are really not so terrible. If they didn't occur, we wouldn't have to meditate in the first place; they are the working ground of our practice. They are the forms our mental energy takes, and we need, in a sense, to accept them. By this I do not mean passively putting up with them; we need to realize that they are going to be there quite a lot of the time and that they have to be acknowledged and dealt with in a creative way. We cannot just push them aside without cutting off a good part of our emotional and mental energy.

The next thing is to have confidence that they can be worked with. The same energy with which we fantasize or worry can, with patience, be engaged with the object of our meditation. The first and most important way to work with these tendencies is to acknowledge them; and the whole point of having this theoretical model is to help us to do that. We train ourselves to put a name to them – 'Oh, there's my old pal Anxiety.' In this way we move from the subjective and associative realm in which they thrive to a more objective realm.

To the degree that we can acknowledge how we really are, we create a part of ourselves that is free from that mental state. We will find that there is nearly always at least a part of us that can see what is going on in a more objective manner. This does not mean splitting ourself off from our experience; rather, it means trying to create a broader context within which to understand the experience. Mental states are very fluid; they change from moment to moment. Awareness means having a sense of continuity above the ever-changing flow of mental states.

Take the way we treat the emotional experience of a young child. A parent seeing a child who is upset knows that half an hour later it will probably have forgotten all about whatever upset it and be restored to a happier state. The child has no such perspective on its own experience and is for that moment consumed by its unhappiness. As we become older we should develop a perspective that allows us not to be quite so engulfed by the passing fluctuations of fortune. However, very often we never really do develop such a sense. Instead, many of us learn not to feel. We learn not to pay attention to our emotions; we cut off from them. In meditation we are trying to relearn how to feel, and acknowledge our feelings but at the same time not be overwhelmed by them. This, in essence, is what compassion in Buddhism is about; it is an ability to feel so deeply that we no longer distinguish between our own feelings and those of others – while at the same time keeping a sense of awareness and clarity.

The hindrances can give tremendous energy to our practice once they become more conscious. There is a story which relates to this, told by a very well-known martial arts expert. She thought of herself as a very able woman, highly trained in self-defence. Then one day she realized that under it all was a great well of fear. It was when she fully realized this that a tremendous energy became available to her as her fear and the energy used to keep her fear down were released. It was not that she no longer had the fear, but that the fear was now available to her and could become integrated into her practice.

So we first have to cultivate the ability to look more objectively at our experience when we meditate. It takes a particular kind of courage or fearlessness to do this. The process of uncovering our mental habits is a long one, but it is very worth while, because these habits inhibit our enjoyment of life and stop us reaching our potential as human beings.

With practice you learn to catch these hindrances before they get a really firm hold on you. It is as though you learn to see them out of the corner of your eye, creeping up on you. This means that you are paying closer attention to your experience. It is increasingly easy to do as you learn to focus the mind, and as your mental activity reduces. It then becomes easier to sense the development of a hindrance and catch it before it comes to dominate the mind.

It is also worth remembering the image of Siddhartha sitting in meditation while under attack from Mara, and the missiles from Mara's army being turned to sweet-scented flowers falling harmlessly around him. We may not manage quite such a transformation, but in the end whatever is happening is just a collection of thoughts and emotions. They have no real power to harm us if we remain alert and centred. We can always stop if it gets too much for us (which is unlikely).

Hindrances occur in varying degrees of strength; they can be very obvious or they can be quite subtle. We will be working with these states, at least in their more subtle forms, for a long time to come. We will become familiar with our own particular favourites. It's best if we don't take them too seriously in a sense. Don't give them a power that in reality they don't have; they will come and go. In one sit they may feel intractable, then in the next we might be completely free from them. Try to keep a sense of humour – no hindrance likes to be laughed at.

So the most important means we have of dealing with these hindrances is simply being aware of them. This means calling them by name. It does not mean trying to unravel them. When we notice we have lost the thread of the practice we can ask ourselves what it is that has taken up our attention, which of the hindrances it is that we are beginning to inhabit; we can name it and then return to the practice. Often this is all we will have to do – frankly admit we are being caught in a distraction and reaffirm our intention to meditate.

Sky-like Attitude

The monks and nuns of Tibet sometimes used to perform a practice in which they lay on their backs and looked at the sky. The sky in Tibet is particularly pure and blue due to the altitude. They would gaze up at the sky for hours on end, imagining that their mind – or rather their consciousness – was as vast as the sky.

In our practice we too can cultivate this experience of unlimited consciousness. When we are troubled by a hindrance we can try to expand around it and give it all the room of the sky. Hindrances are contractive by nature; they have a feeling of closing down. We tend to collapse into them. Expand your awareness into the body, think of the hindrance as a passing cloud, let it go on its way. This is not the same as completely ignoring it – we acknowledge it and go forward.

I am reminded of a wonderful little routine by Richard Pryor, the black comic, imitating a white man walking through the jungle and encountering a snake. He is completely freaked out and leaps two foot into the air, squealing 'Snake! Snake!' He then shows a black man encountering the same snake. The black man sees the snake and doesn't miss a step. He just gives it a little wave, smiles, says 'Hi snake,' and strolls on.

The snake in this case is one of the five hindrances. When we spot it we can over-react or we can just notice it and move on. We try not to excite it by shrieking and jumping out of our skin. We try to allow our experience to broaden out, connecting with a sense of the vastness of the mind that is all around the worry or the craving, both in space and time. With this we counteract the tendency to fall into a contracted state centred around the hindrance.

We can deliberately bring attention to our posture, relax the body, and have a sense of the breath. In this way we try to create a sense of space that includes the hindrance without being focused on it. You can see why this is called a sky-like attitude; instead of pushing the hindrance away we expand around it.

Cultivating the Opposite

If we have acknowledged the hindrance and tried to let it go, but it still hangs around, then we might need to try something a little more active. One thing we can do is consciously cultivate the positive emotion opposite to it. This can be done in a number of ways – by using thought, or by working through the body, or by a combination of the two.

It is sometimes helpful to see the hindrance in terms of the quality of its energy. Some hindrances, such as anxiety, or ill will, or craving, may well have a high energy to them (though they don't always) in which case we will tend to feel as though our energy is high up in the body. We can work against these hindrances by trying to ground our energy in the body, bring it back to base, calm it down. We can bring our awareness to a sense of being 'earthed', or take our attention to the sensations of contact with the ground, and be aware of the breathing deep down. With hindrances which have a dull, low energy tone to them, we need to get our energy moving again by bringing our awareness higher up in the body. We need to encourage a sense of energy starting to flow, and even bubbling, to allow the hindrance to move on.

To a greater or lesser degree, the body will manifest the hindrances in some way or other – so learn to use your body to help counter them. Just softening one's face is sometimes enough to allow one to let go of feelings of hatred. And just bringing up the head and opening the chest can be enough to wake one up and brighten one's awareness.

Over time we will get to know the character of our own customary distractions. If we are constantly prey to ill will, we might want to concentrate our efforts for a while on the first stage of the Metta Bhavana. If we experience a lot of restlessness and anxiety, we can be aware of this tendency before we start the practice, and perhaps make a list of all the things we are likely to worry about and keep it for later. Then we can make sure that we spend an appropriate amount of time settling the body with a body meditation. And during the meditation we can use initial or sustained thought to promote a sense of calm.

Hindrances have to be worked with over time, not just in a piecemeal fashion. And it is true to say that the meditations them-selves are the best antidote to the hindrances. Over time the hin-drances are diminished by our sincere efforts to develop positive emotional qualities. The practices are themselves the cultivation of the opposite qualities to the hindrances, so the best thing we can do is to return to the practice as often as possible.

This might mean that we have to go back and start over again and again, but every time we reconnect with the practice we are working against the hindrances. This is a very simple point and relates to the idea of intention that we discussed before. It is very simple but easily forgotten. If you feel you are getting lost in a hindrance – stop! Open your eyes for a second, take a couple of deeper breaths, and remind yourself what your purpose is. Say to yourself 'I am trying to practise the Mindfulness of Breathing,' re-establish the intention to do that, and start again.

Considering the Consequences

At some point we will see that we are free of a hindrance. We can examine it critically and see through it, or put it to one side. If something left undone is causing us anxiety, we can acknowledge that we need to get it done, and that we will attend to it after the meditation. I have known people who find it useful to have a pen and paper with them to write down what is bugging them, and then they find it easier to get back to the practice.

If we don't manage to get back to the practice, we might want to follow through in our minds where this hindrance is leading us – while keeping an objective distance from it. If we can become a bit more aware of what we are getting caught up in, we can stimulate a distaste for it – because much of the power of hindrances comes from our ease with them; we feel at home with them. So we need to take an unsqueamish look at what they are really up to.

Do we really want to indulge our capacity for ill will? Doing so is not a neutral act, because every time we allow this tendency to take us over we are strengthening it. If we sit in a state of ill will we are cultivating that particular mental habit. We can ask ourselves 'What would I be like if I just let myself become dominated by this emotion? Is that what I really want to be like?' We might try bringing to mind an image of ourselves as angry and bad-tempered. What does a bitter and resentful person look like? What does that state of mind really feel like? Is that what we want to be?

The fact that we have taken the trouble to meditate at all shows us that this is not really what we want. So just for a few seconds we can see in our mind's eye an image of where the hindrance could take us, and by doing so strengthen our desire to transform the negative emotion. Just how safe and secure do we have to be before we can relax and stop worrying? Is there really going to be some point in the future when everything is OK and we can just smile at life; or is the last thing we experience in life before the heart attack hits us going to be yet another niggling worry? Do we value life so little that we want to hide away in fantasy or somnolence? When are we going to have a full, alive, authentic experience of ourselves? Just how long are we going to do things by half before we decide to go for it?

Suppression

This should be used sparingly. It does have a place if we are fairly sure that what we are dealing with is a 'covering' hindrance – if, that is, we feel there is some other more basic problem underneath. This is often the case with restlessness. It is a good idea simply to learn to sit still, unless one is in pain. If we suppress the hindrance on this level we will often bring its underlying cause more clearly out into the open.

Suppression can also be very useful in the case of minor irritations. For example, if a recording of Julie Andrews singing 'My Favourite Things' is playing in your head, just suppress it – or at least see if you can switch it to something more subtle, like John Coltrane or Bach.

This raises the interesting question of 'When is a hindrance really a hindrance?' I'm afraid there's no easy answer. It would be wrong to have too rigid a view of the practices; we have to allow for the creativity of the mind to enrich our meditation, and sometimes it can do that in unexpected ways. So we can identify 'My Favourite Things' as the manifestation of a hindrance, but it is quite possible that recreating a beautiful piece of music in the imagination could stimulate us in the right direction.

Up to a point you have to trust your gut feelings. Sometimes you will be wrong, and that's fine as long as you try to learn from it. I think that bearing in mind the basic tone of the hindrances is helpful: you can ask yourself 'Does this feel conducive to mindful states, to feelings of loving-kindness?' In the end you have to go with what you feel, but also retain a sense of what it is you are trying to do.

Going for Refuge

Traditionally, there is one last method for dealing with distractions in meditation. I have left it to the end as it is rather different from the others. The term 'Going for Refuge' refers to the act that makes someone a Buddhist; it is the conscious decision of the individual to follow the Buddhist path to the exclusion of other ways of life. That is to say, the individual decides that spiritual development is the prime goal of their life (before, say, making money or having a family) and that the Buddhist tradition is the vehicle for such development.

So if such a person is finding meditation difficult they will reaffirm their commitment to the Buddhist path of transformation. In this way, a difficult meditation, or period of time in which meditation seems to be difficult, is put into perspective. One is reminding oneself that one's undertaking to move towards spiritual maturity is a long-term one that will take time and effort. In this way one re-establishes one's desire to persist through periods that seem fruitless.

Strictly speaking, this method applies only to someone who has 'gone for Refuge', but it can be of help to us all. If we cannot remind ourselves that we have gone for Refuge, we at least can remind ourselves that, in the past, meditation has been both useful and enjoyable. We can remember and stimulate our desire for positive change. We can reaffirm our wish to develop and try to see a difficult session of meditation in the overall, long-term scheme of working on ourselves.

Traditionally, Going for Refuge is the most direct way of dealing with doubt and indecision, as it consists in the cultivation of the opposite quality to that hindrance – the cultivation of resolution and confidence in our own potential. Just as doubt can be said to underlie all the other hindrances, so this quality of confidence – despite the ups and downs that are sure to occur – can be said to underpin a successful long-term practice of meditation. It is not easy to get a long-term view of our practice, but it is worth developing.

Imagine meditating every morning for ten years, every morning spending time developing awareness and metta. It is bound to have a profound effect, even if you struggle most of the time. Because you are making that effort, you are going to be a very different person from what you would otherwise have been. What we do affects us. This is a simple but vital truth. If we freely indulge the negative aspects of ourselves they will grow. If we consciously encourage the positive aspects, even sporadically, they will increase.

This is our basic choice as self-aware beings. We can recreate ourselves, or we can allow the negative forces within and without to mould us in their likeness. When we affirm our commitment to meditation we are affirming what is most human and valuable in ourselves – the desire and ability to change in a self-conscious and positive manner. This is surely the overriding value of human life. It is what makes us truly human.

The Challenge of Meditation

Clearly, the hindrances come in all shapes and sizes, so we need a wide range of antidotes to them. Some hindrances are fairly superficial and just catching sight of them can be enough to move them on. Others, however, have their roots deep down in well-established emotional attitudes about ourselves and the world. When working in meditation with these more deep-rooted tendencies we must retain a sense of metta towards ourselves. I sometimes think of this as being like our attitude towards a person we hold very dear. We might see their faults very clearly, we might even try to help them overcome them, but we do so with an attitude of care and concern – we don't threaten or bully them.

The thing to remember is that you cannot deal with these distractions on their own level; you cannot overcome ill will by feeling more ill will towards yourself on account of the original ill will. The practices themselves create a context in which we can more fully experience the habits of mind that make us up. In the end it is awareness, in the sense of clarity of experience, that helps us over-come – or rather transform – the hindrance.

The different ways of dealing with these distractions I have been describing are really just simple techniques we can employ to help us bring an increased and directed awareness into our experience. They are not magic bullets. They won't work in a mechanical way to get rid of our distractions. We need to have a realistic sense that little of our meditation is going to consist of enjoyable floods of metta. Most of the time it is going to be a matter of working in a creative way with the aspects of ourselves that inhibit our ability to feel metta.

This is the real challenge of meditation. It is not about being in exalted trance-like states; it is about working creatively with our everyday consciousness. Slowly, over the weeks, months, and years, we are encouraging and developing our ability to feel joy, take delight, enjoy what we are. The five categories we have been looking at are there to help us deepen our awareness of the emotional texture of the distraction. In this sense, working with distraction is an inherent part of the meditation experience.

Through seeing more deeply into the nature of the hindrance we are also getting to know ourselves more deeply, so the hindrance can actually give us revealing insights. We can then return to the point of our practice which is the direct cultivation of positive mental and emotional states.

Often a less direct approach to the hindrances works best. Concentrate on the positive, encouraging a sense of confidence and self-worth. In meditation we can get too caught up with the difficulties and fail to notice the positive elements. Meditation is not a form of self-analysis. We do not have to undo all our psychological complexes in order to progress in meditation.

The Buddhist view is rather different from the way most forms of psychotherapy see things. From a Buddhist point of view our negative tendencies do not ultimately have an identifiable beginning. It is true that our conditioning can strengthen or weaken them; we can have a traumatic childhood, say, that firmly establishes in us a powerful and individual configuration of one of these negative emotions. We may even need psychotherapy to deal with it. But in the context of meditation the hindrances should be understood and addressed as general negative tendencies which are part of our lot as human beings.

The practices themselves are designed to promote well-being and mental health. Give them a try. See what happens if you just trust in the practice.

Now let's have a look at the other side of meditation – the development of the positive factors within our meditative experience.

nine

THE POSITIVE FACTORS

Perhaps even more important than being aware of what can distract you from your meditation practice is paying attention to those aspects of your experience that support and encourage the cultivation of awareness and metta. Our approach to our practice should be as balanced as possible. So we should pay at least as much attention to the enjoyable elements of our experience as we do to the difficulties.

Over the years I've spent teaching, I've begun to feel that for many people the very idea of the hindrances can be a bit of a hindrance. Many people seem to be inclined to a rather more problematic approach to meditation than is useful. As I have tried to indicate, one way to counteract this is to view the hindrances not as unwelcome visitors but as opportunities to engage with the practice.

However, even if we are able to see them in this light and maintain a sense of creativity in dealing with them, we will still need to pay close attention to the other side of our experience. I have already talked quite a bit about the positive factors in looking at balancing energy in meditation. But it's a good time now, after all that talk about the hindrances, to focus on them more thoroughly.

We can only work with what is actually there in our experience. There is no magic method to go from a distracted, anxious state of mind to a calm, serene one. We might have heard stories about great meditators who slip effortlessly into sublime ecstasy at the drop of a hat. And maybe such people do exist. But what we tend to forget is that such abilities are based, in nearly all cases, on many years of dedicated meditation practice. The Zen monk who gains Enlightenment when he hears a pebble hitting a bamboo fence has spent the last thirty years sitting eight hours a day, every day, in a draughty Zendo.

For most of us, each practice means taking account of how we are and creatively using what is there in order to move slowly towards a more aware and positive state. We are, then, like sculptors faced with a crudely hewn block of stone, knowing that the stone has a wonderful figure locked within it. Each time we take up our chisel we try to unlock the potential we can sense waiting to be released. And, like a sculptor, we have to take into account the basic characteristics of the stone.

Through meditation we become ourselves, not somebody different. The essential elements of our personality do not disappear. They are simply reorganized so that they work better. There is a lot of misunderstanding about the process of change involved in the Buddhist idea of development. There is a lot of talk about getting rid of the self. But what does this really mean? What is a person without a self? When such ideas are understood in a superficial way they are very misleading and confusing.

The stories about the Buddha make it clear that he had a very strong personality. He had, one could say, a strong sense of self. He was certainly not some spaced-out, vacant guy walking around with an inane smile on his face. We can say that he had seen through the idea of a fixed self and had gone beyond acting from ordinary, limited, self-centredness. But he was still himself. He was, we could say, a true individual; he no longer needed to bolster up his idea of self or to conform to others' ideas of what he should be or do. He was able to respond creatively to whatever confronted him, because he was both objective and compassionate.

The point is that it is far more useful – at least to begin with – to think in terms of creating a positive self than to think of getting rid of or eradicating the self. Furthermore, it is helpful to feel that all the elements of a positive self are already there within us. It is just a matter of reorganizing them, getting them to work together so that they can manifest more and more strongly.

To do this we can't just rely on meditation; we have to practise in our everyday lives, in our interaction with others. But it is within meditation that we get the chance to see most clearly what we need to do. Meditation is a space we create in our busy lives to take stock of ourselves, to come home and be with what we are. A life without such a space is a life devoid of the sacred, a life in which our spiritual aspects have little chance to manifest.

In our early years we are not self-aware enough to make conscious decisions and sustain the effort that is needed to bring about changes in ourselves. Anyway, we are changing so fast under the forces of biology and socialization that it is more than we can do just to keep up with what is going on. But slowly we gain an increased awareness that we can be more than just passive actors reading the scripts that have been written for us by biological or social forces.

Unfortunately, many of us never act on this awareness, which may become increasingly dimmed as we lose touch with the sense of possibility we had when young. We don't know how we lose touch with it, but maybe we just go along with the path that presents itself, and our lives are always shadowed by a more or less conscious sense that we are not fulfilling our destiny. We might even appear to others to be very much in control of our lives, doing what we really want to do. But somewhere inside we perhaps know that we have never made a sustained effort to develop, and that despite the appearance of a successful life we remain in essence a passive child of fortune.

Modern society has all but given up on the idea that the individual can recreate his or her self – an idea that used to be called growing up. For example, the so-called American dream – once a dream motivated by ideals of individual and social development, by high ideals of freedom and fraternity – is now a nightmare of untrammelled consumption and greed. We are kept like children, our primary function to consume – food, entertainment, and, if we are clever children, ideas. But we are never satisfied because, like children, we have a need to grow up. Our real hunger is for a deeper connection with ourselves, with others, with the world around us, and with reality.

The opening lines of Walt Whitman's poem 'Song of Myself' strongly evoke not only the original robust spiritual energy of American culture but also a sense of tremendous human possibility. They also beautifully evoke the spirit of metta.

> I celebrate myself, and sing myself,
> And what I assume you shall assume,
> For every atom belonging to me as good belongs to you.
>
> I loafe and invite my soul,
> I lean and loafe at my ease observing a spear of summer
> grass.
>
> My tongue, every atom of my blood, form'd from this soil,
> this air,
> Born here of parents born here from parents the same, and

their parents the same,
>   I, now thirty-seven years old in perfect health begin,
>   Hoping to cease not till death.

Meditation is the first step to taking care of what is most of value in us, our capacity for kindness and clarity, our capacity to enjoy and appreciate ourselves, others, and the world, to feel a deep relatedness to life. This movement begins at the centre. It begins in a simple and direct way by the conscious nurturing of the best in ourselves. We learn to identify and cultivate the positive aspects in our own experience. Within the context of meditation these are known as the five positive factors of meditation: initial thought, sustained thought, rapture, bliss, and one-pointedness.

Initial and Sustained Thought

We have dealt with these in some detail with regard to working in meditation. But these two ways of using thought are not just useful aids to becoming concentrated. They are in themselves elements of a concentrated state. I want to emphasize this, as it contradicts a lot of the popular notions about meditation. We could go so far as to say that the experience of clear directed thought is the most important element in meditation. It is in itself positive.

This may become clearer if we look at the traditional way of describing levels of meditative concentration. There are basically four of these, called the *dhyanas* (though the fourth may be divided into four further dhyanas). We reach the first of these when we are free from gross distractions. We feel the mind becoming absorbed into the object of meditation, with the normally dispersed elements of our experience gathering around the object. This first level of concentration, which is the gateway to higher levels, is marked predominantly by clarity of thought – thought that is related to the meditation practice.

So thought in the sense of initial thought and sustained thought is the foundation of concentration. This first dhyana also contains the other positive factors of meditation, but these first two are the prevailing ones. It is therefore necessary to cultivate thought in order to move towards deeper levels of meditation where thought is left behind.

This ability to think clearly and in a directed manner is also one of the most useful of the qualities that meditation encourages. We become increasingly able to turn the mind where we want it to go, bringing a sense of brightness and clarity to our experience. This kind of thinking is also enjoyable, in that we feel the flexibility and creative responsiveness of the mind. It is not at all a dry, heady rationality, because it has developed within a context in which other positive factors are developing.

Rapture

According to the model of the four dhyanas, as thought begins to become more subtle so the experience of rapture increases. The second dhyana has this experience of rapture at its core. Traditionally, rapture is said to range from mildly pleasant sensations to feelings so intense and powerful that they can cause the body to leave the ground.

When I first began to meditate I experienced a lot of pleasant sensations in the body – feelings of quite intense energy moving around. I decided they were distractions and tried to ignore them and dampen them down. I was not then aware that they were, in fact, a manifestation of the positive process of integration that occurs in meditation.

It is not uncommon to experience such sensations of rapture early on in our practice, so we should look out for them and enjoy them. They might develop out of a simple feeling of relaxation in the body, or a feeling of warmth, or an opening up of the body. We can therefore encourage this development by paying attention to those quite simple experiences.

We should not, however, try to force out or grab at these feelings of rapture. This does not really work. Just relax into them when they come and enjoy them for what they are. They will come and go. Trying to hold on to them will only hasten their departure. They have nothing to do with any sense of clinging on to things. They are positive in themselves because they are often associated with the body relaxing, the dissipation of tension, and the release of blocks in the body. But they also have the positive function of giving the mind something relatively refined to engage with, and of fuelling positive mental states.

It seems that some people are more inclined to rapture than others, but it is not so much the intensity of these feelings as our sensitivity to them that is important. When we are in a concentrated state we are more able to enjoy the pleasant sensations in our body that are occurring all the time. The hands are a wonderful place to begin to get a sense of the energy and vitality of the body. It is this sense of the life within us that forms the basis for the arising of rapture within our meditation.

So we can see that these factors of meditation begin to fit together: a clear, flexible mind will be able to be aware of the elements of rapture in our experience. Directing the mind to these elements will also encourage the mind to become engaged with our present experience. Our thoughts will become finer – there is still mental activity, but it is light and spacious, as the mind becomes increasingly engaged in this way. The elements of bliss will strengthen, moving us towards the third dhyana.

Bliss

The experience of bliss is a result of our physical and mental experience becoming more deeply integrated. Again, bliss has many levels. It begins with a simple contentment in being occupied with our direct experience of the object of meditation, and can grow into intense feelings of ecstatic or serene joy. It is different from rapture in that it is not associated so much with the body as with the mind.

While full-blown bliss is not an everyday occurrence for most of us, we should encourage its seeds by promoting contentment in our practice. Sometimes such experiences can happen suddenly: one moment we are involved in a seemingly intractable hindrance and the next we have flipped the energy of the hindrance over. High energy hindrances in particular have the potential to become experiences of bliss. We give up resisting the hindrance in a wilful way, just manage to bring awareness to it, and transform the nature of the energy.

In order to meditate effectively, we have to develop what for many people is a completely different attitude towards ourselves and to what is and is not worth doing. In today's society we have what seems to be a more and more utilitarian attitude towards life. We are supposed to make ourselves useful, to be busy. Traditionally, Buddhism turns the idea of laziness on its head, in that it defines laziness as the pursuit of power and material wealth. Worthwhile activity is oriented towards spiritual growth and the creation of a society where positive human values hold sway.

To develop contentment does not mean becoming passive. When we begin to find that just being with our breath can bring about states of great happiness and calm, we also begin to question what we should really be valuing. Western society is now based on the twin values of wealth and romantic love, both of which tend to cut us off from one another, from a wider sense of fellowship, of feeling part of a community. The ideal of wealth involves dividing ourselves from the poor; while the romantic ideal is so overloaded with having to carry all our human emotional needs that it all too easily splits at the seams and breaks down.

Many of us are caught up in a desperate search for one or both of these ideals. But life is not something that is suddenly going to start happening when we find these things. It is happening now, from moment to moment. Contentment is not something we will find in the future. It is now – we either consciously try to develop it now or we do not. To think that events outside us over which we have little control are going to bring it about is a bit unrealistic.

So a simple sense of contentment – that is, being happy to be with our concrete experience – forms the basis for the arising of bliss. The cultivation of this quality means that we don't stand outside waiting for life to happen to us. When we experience for ourselves that sitting quietly with the breath, or encouraging metta, can be a source of great contentment our attitude towards what life has to offer us changes. We begin to tune in to the relationship between simplicity and depth – that it is in fact the simplest parts of life which hold the most potential for a deeper experience of contentment and bliss.

A popular misconception is that depth of experience is something to do with intensity of experience. We crave strong feelings through experiences that stimulate adrenaline – so-called 'peak experiences' – that leave us with a further craving for excitement. It is considered, apparently, that these kinds of experience gained through vividly exciting – often sexual – activities, represent the best and most fulfilling things that life has to offer. In fact, of course, they are just fun – which is OK, but we can't expect them to satisfy our need for meaning and value. Fun – even exquisite fun – can afford no more than a superficial and temporary relief to jaded senses.

In meditation the development of contentment is linked to encouraging our ability to feel deeply. It is only on the foundation of a clear, relatively integrated mind that experience will penetrate deeply.

One-pointedness

The positive factors we have been looking at all have their source in the gradual and increasing bringing together of our mental and emotional energies around the object of concentration. This gathering of ourselves is the factor known as one-pointedness. Its emotional equivalent is the equanimity we have already talked about. One-pointedness is to some degree always present in our waking life. In essence it is what we call self-consciousness. But as a dhyanic factor this has been refined to a high degree.

If we manage to keep deepening our experience we will find that bliss begins to subside and we enter a calmer, vibrant state. At this point all the positive factors are blended together or – we may even say – absorbed. In this sense, one-pointedness grows out of the other factors, it is a harmonization and a stabilization of them. As a meditative state it is extremely refined, for it represents a stage where all our psycho-physical energies are focused in subtle experience of the object of meditation.

This is quite difficult to explain in words, as in a sense 'we' do not any longer experience the object as separate from us. The 'we' part of the experience has fallen away. However, we can encourage one-pointedness at an early stage in our practice by developing as strong an interest as we can in the object of concentration. This really is not so different from what can happen in daily life.

Say you are talking to someone. If you allow yourself to be distracted into thinking about other things you are soon going to feel bored. On the other hand, if you give that person your full attention, the communication can often take on a quite different aspect. It deepens, and you end up feeling that you have had a worthwhile conversation.

I know from experience that people who come to meditation classes are often struck by the fact that people at the classes take an interest in each other. Sometimes people have said to me that it was the first time in their lives that they felt listened to. People blossom when they are listened to. This is not the kind of gushing super-friendliness that feels like treacle is being poured over you. It simply means having time for each other.

The same is true of our meditation practice – we have to feel that we have time for it; we have to take a real interest in it. This does not mean being passive, or having an idea about what we would like to be experiencing. As with other people we can only make the practice work if we are prepared to give up, to some extent, an idea of wanting something from the interaction. If we want something we are not prepared just to listen, to be with what is there.

While it would be unrealistic to expect that you will always manage to attain the first dhyana, let alone the higher dhyanas, it is nevertheless useful to bear the five positive factors in mind every time you meditate, and to encourage their presence. These factors are really another way of talking about balance in meditation, albeit on a slightly more refined level.

These factors should not be seen as strictly sequential. You don't need to have experienced intense rapture to be aware of elements of bliss; nor do you have to establish a state of bliss before you can be aware of elements of one-pointedness. Although these factors might sound rather exalted, they are often present to some degree just in normal life. When we respond strongly to a piece of music or a beautiful landscape, there are elements of rapture. When we feel a sense of contentment, of fulfilment, in life, there are elements of bliss in that. So these factors are not really all that exotic. They are just part of our emotional capacity as human beings, but experienced more fully and completely because of the concentration in which they are experienced. In meditation, paying closer attention to them and discovering our own capacity to develop them, we strengthen our ability to experience them and our experience of them becomes more concentrated.

ten

INSIGHT

At the beginning of this book I talked a little about the two broad groups into which meditation practices are often classified: *samatha*, or tranquillity meditations, and *vipassana*, or insight meditations. *Samatha* meditation is seen as a means of preparing the ground for the seeds of insight to take root.

The term 'insight' is used in a particular way within the Buddhist tradition. It does not refer to psychological insights, or the sudden feeling that we have gained a clearer understanding of something. Insight in Buddhism means a fundamental shift in the way that we view ourselves and the world around us. It is not merely an intellectual understanding, however profound, but rather a turning about, as it is said, in the very depths of our being.

There are many ways of talking about the nature of insight within the Buddhist tradition. One of the most straightforward is to view it as the direct experience of how things are – in particular, the direct experience of the impermanent nature of things.

If we apply this general truth to ourselves, it means that we begin more and more to give up ideas about ourselves as fixed and separate, as having some essential and unchanging core, and begin to experience ourselves as a means of connection, as part of the whole flow of being. Clearly it is very difficult to articulate the nature of such insight, because it is beyond the range of normal human experience. The only knowledge we can have of it is direct experience.

In a sense, we have all we need to experience insight already. We have highly developed senses with which we can see, hear, touch, smell, taste the world – and in fact the experience of our senses is that of impermanence. Nothing can be held by the senses for very long. We also have our ability to be aware of ourselves, and again we find thoughts and moods and fancies that come and go. On the other hand we seem to have a kind of basic ignorance, a very strong inclination towards self-delusion, a refusal to believe what is before our eyes.

We cannot *make* ourselves experience insight. We can only encourage the internal and external conditions that will support its arising. But if we do this we have to be prepared for a complete turnaround in the way we normally view ourselves and the world. We move from experiencing ourselves as separate from reality to experiencing ourselves as part of reality. We move from a state where we crave love to one where we radiate love, from a fear of change to a deeper understanding and appreciation of impermanence.

We might remember the Buddha-to-be seated deep in meditation on the brink of Enlightenment, all his fears and cravings falling away, falling as beautiful blossoms around his serene figure. We might imagine, as far as we could, a great sense of calm pervading his mind as the understanding of how things are in reality penetrated to the very core of his being – to such a degree that never again would he feel at odds with his own existence. We might see him sitting there, his longing for meaning and understanding of life being fully satisfied by a complete embracing of the nature of existence.

In this image we can perhaps get a sense of the nature of insight, which is at one and the same time a profound individual experience and a direct perception of a universal truth. Opportunities to cultivate insight abound. The simplest thing is pregnant with reality. There is nothing we can contemplate that does not remind us of the basic nature of everything.

However, certain experiences are clearly more powerful in their ability to promote insight that others. Any experience that shakes us to the roots, be it pleasant or unpleasant, provides the opportunity to approach nearer to an understanding of reality. Yet even something like the death of a loved one does not often cause any permanent change in our deluded state.

The Tibetans have a saying that puts this rather well. They say that you cannot wake up someone who is only pretending to be asleep. In a sense we are all pretending to be ignorant of the nature of reality. In our culture we have a mass conspiracy to keep it at arm's length. We treat death as though it is a surprise occurrence, a terrible aberration, a freak happening that really shouldn't take place in a civilized society. Of course we know we are going to die, but we don't accept it on a deeper level. There's another saying – 'Death comes to everyone – me too, maybe.'

This unacknowledged fear of death prevents us from really living. It stops us from attending to what really matters to us, stops us from really connecting with one another. Over the last few years I have been a volunteer at a hospice, and I chose to do this because I wanted to come into closer contact with the reality of death. But even though I have now seen the process of death happening to many people, I can still feel my own resistance to fully taking on the fact of my own impermanence. It is for most of us a slow process of chipping away at our own delusion.

Both the meditations we have learned can help us not only to integrate ourselves so as to increase the possibility that insight will find ground in us, but also to encourage insight more directly. The Metta Bhavana slowly promotes an attitude of connectedness with others. It helps us to move away from a position of self-centredness to one of emotional generosity. We begin to experience our communality with others rather than our separateness. Paradoxically, it is through cultivating the ability to appreciate people in their full individual richness and uniqueness that we also appreciate what is common to all life, and develop a deep sympathy with life in all its manifestations. We realize, in Sangharakshita's phrase, that 'life is king'.

We have talked about metta mainly as a positive emotion. This is a useful way of seeing it, but rather a limited one. As our practice of metta deepens we will begin to see that it is not simply an emotion in the normal sense of that term. It is not just a matter of feeling good about ourselves and others. What we are promoting in the practice is a dramatic shift in the way we see the world and our place in it. We are slowly encouraging an emotional expansion which will need to be supported by a shift in attitude.

We are moving from a state where our attitude towards the world is based in selfishness to one based in altruism. But this change takes place not because we are able to overcome selfishness in the sense of overcoming 'sin', but because we slowly begin to see that our selfishness is based in a delusion about the nature of existence itself. This delusion has at its root the notion that we are somehow separate, self-contained entities, and that our best interests can be separated from the general good. The practice of the Metta Bhavana helps us to move beyond this attitude by promoting a strong but flexible view of ourselves. We begin to feel less threatened by others, we begin to see that other people are not so different from us, that at heart we all seek to be happy. And we begin to realize that this happiness we seek cannot be gained at the expense of others.

In Mahayana Buddhism, the second major historical development of Buddhism, the central image of the Buddhist practitioner changes from that of the monk or nun to that of the bodhisattva. The bodhisattva is someone who conceives of their spiritual life above all in terms of altruism. Their personal practice is oriented towards developing the qualities that can be used to help others; their life is one of service to others. Now this shift in emphasis does not mean that Mahayana Buddhists stopped being concerned about their own development, or that other Buddhists were selfish. It came about because the development of this altruistic emphasis was seen to be simply more effective, in the sense that it was more congruent with the nature of how things really are – as well as being more inspiring.

We therefore need to find concrete ways in which the emotions we are developing in the Metta Bhavana can be expressed in an ordinary human way. In the end it is not enough just to wish others well; we need also to express this wish in selfless action. Here the notion of service is useful. Our lives need to contain an element of service, action that is performed for the benefit of others. Such service does not mean beginning to see ourselves as spiritual social workers; it means finding something we can do that is of practical help to others.

This might be, say, cleaning house for a disabled person. I once rather upset a friend by suggesting that he would do more good as a garbage collector than as a psychotherapist. By this I was trying to point out that what we think of as useful is often conditioned by ideas of social status and prestige. If we really want to be of service to others, we do best to think of practical, everyday things – doing the shopping, cooking a meal, and so on.

Being of service means placing ourselves at the disposal of others, not putting ourselves in a position in which we are telling them what's wrong or what they should do. If we have the time it is of great benefit, to ourselves, to find a volunteer position where we can express in a down-to-earth way the attitude that we are trying to develop in our practice. I say this sort of thing is of great benefit to ourselves because it is, but of course we won't get very far if that is our sole motivation. Benefiting others needs to become an end in itself, beyond the pleasure and benefit we derive from it ourselves.

So the Metta Bhavana is chipping away at the emotional attitudes that inhibit us from seeing the world as it really is. The insight element of the practice is enhanced if we take time to reflect on the practice and our experience of feeling metta. With this reflection we support the practical application of metta in action; and this action will act back on the practice and deepen our understanding and experience of metta.

It is a very radical practice indeed – the idea that it is possible to move in the direction of a life lived for the good of all. Normally we see this sort of altruism in terms of self-sacrifice, but this is not the case here. A life dedicated to the good of all, if it is based on positive emotion and awareness – rather than 'do-gooding' or fear or duty or obedience or conscious humility – will prove to be a source of great joy and contentment.

In the mindfulness practice we can have a direct experience of ourselves as an ever-changing expression of life. We can feel our breath coming and going like the ocean on the shore, experience the impermanence of our thoughts and feelings, and begin to get a sense of the unlimited nature of our consciousness. As we deepen our experience of this meditation we will become aware that sometimes we are free from thoughts – that gaps in the constant succession of thoughts are appearing.

At first, these gaps may be a little disconcerting. We will realize we are free from thoughts, and with that realization we will realize we have found a new thought to fill the gap. But as time goes on we will become more comfortable with allowing a sense of spaciousness to enter our experience. We will realize we don't have to think all the time. Our sense of self is so bound up with perpetual mental activity that when it first starts to decrease we can feel as though we are losing our ground. It is a little as though we take Descartes' dictum 'I think, therefore I am' literally – fearing that if we stopped thinking we would stop existing.

Mindfulness is really the ability to be fully aware of a situation without having to add anything to it. There is a famous teaching of the Buddha, on hearing which a disciple called Bahiya of the Bark Garment gained transcendental insight. It comes from the *Udana* – a collection of the Buddha's teachings.

> Then, Bahiya, thus must you train yourself: In the seen
> there will be just the seen, in the heard just the heard, in
> the imagined just the imagined, in the cognized just the
> cognized. Thus you will have no 'thereby'. That is how you
> must train yourself. Now, Bahiya, when in the seen there
> will be to you just the seen, in the heard just the heard, in
> the imagined just the imagined, in the cognized just the
> cognized, then, Bahiya, as you will have no 'thereby', you
> will have no 'therein'. As you, Bahiya, will have no
> 'therein', it follows that you will have no 'here' or 'beyond'
> or 'midway between'. That is just the end of Ill.

To experience things in this bare way calls for a clear and limpid mind, one that has overcome the habitual tendency to add to our experience, to impose a sense of 'I' between ourselves and the experience. There is only the experience. This ability to 'experience' within a clear, vast awareness, free from the limitations of views and thoughts about ourselves, is encouraged particularly by the practice of mindfulness.

With the development of more refined states of mind through meditation, we can begin moving towards being able to take a long look at the true nature of reality without feeling we will be overwhelmed by it. We become less fearful of experiencing a sense of spaciousness, of making room for insights to penetrate more deeply. So when opportunities for insight arise we are less inclined to turn away from them. We feel less threatened by the fact of impermanence, and begin to see that it is impermanence that makes life possible, which makes life worth living at all.

I remember many years ago, before I became interested in Buddhism, having a discussion with two Jehovah's Witnesses. They were telling me about the after-life, about what one could look forward to as a good Jehovah's Witness. Their ideal seemed to be an unchanging, perfectly landscaped world with perfect weather. But if we really imagine a world without change it doesn't seem to be at all attractive. The glory of life is in its movement and change, its growth and decay, and the new life that comes out of decay. Whether it is in the slow explosion and dissolution of universes (slow, of course, to us) or in the life of a mayfly (brief to us) we find everywhere this constant turning over of life into death and then back again in another form, another expression; until it becomes clear that what we are looking at is the nature of reality.

Within the Zen tradition the moment of Enlightenment is sometimes likened to the turning over of a large carp in crystal clear water.

The water offers no resistance, but supports the effortless movement of the fish in its natural element. As it turns, light strikes the scales, refracting into rainbow light, and for an instant the fish is made purely of beautiful light.

This image points to the paradox of spiritual aspiration. After many years of practice, insights can occur at any time, and under the most mundane circumstances. They flash upon the mind out of nowhere. However, our ability to integrate such insights so that they truly permeate our whole being has to be diligently cultivated, over years.

When we have an experience which has the flavour of insight, we need to give it the time and space to get properly in amongst us. We can do this by turning the insight over in the mind when we are concentrated in meditation. It's not so much that we 'think' about it in the normal sense. It's not that we analyse it, or mentally squeeze it. It's more that we just hold it in a clear and positive attentiveness. Our normal level of awareness is not capable of this – if it were, we should already have achieved insight. Only awareness free from its normal, habitual ways of thinking can help us here. We sometimes talk about knowing something in our guts. Well, insight is knowing – no, experiencing – our own essential nature (which is the nature of reality itself) not only in our guts but in every living fibre of our whole being.

eleven

SETTING UP AND MAINTAINING YOUR PRACTICE

Setting up your Practice

What happens in our meditation is largely a function of the mental states we bring to it. Meditation is simply the crucible within which certain of our mental states can act upon others. At Buddhist centres where meditation is taught we try to create an atmosphere that is supportive of people's practice. When we come to meditate at home we should also do what we can to give ourselves the best chance of having a useful meditation.

If you get up from watching junk television programmes and dump yourself in the middle of the floor, in a bad posture and a bad mood, for a few minutes' meditation before the next programme, you are not giving yourself a chance. What we do outside meditation supplies us with what we work with in it, so it's a good idea to regard the closest elements of that context – your preparation and your approach – as part of your practice.

Not many of us have the space to have a separate room in our house for meditation, but we can probably find, say, a suitable corner of a room. I often encourage people to set up a modest shrine. By this I mean a visual focus for one's meditation. It might simply be a postcard pinned to a wall, a picture that symbolizes what you are trying to move towards in meditation. Often people add a couple of candles and fresh flowers, and burn incense. This sort of thing creates a space which is to some extent separated from our daily living environment. Maybe the rest of our bedroom is a bit of a mess, but we have just a corner that we keep free of clutter for our meditation. The lighting of candles and incense also helps us to feel that we are entering a different realm, a place dedicated to the development of awareness and loving-kindness. It helps to facilitate a movement from the everyday world, and the states of mind that predominate in that world, to a more creative and even magical world of transformations.

We will find that having a simple shrine helps to remind us to practise. Over the years, people's shrines tend to grow. My own has not only a couple of traditional Buddhist images but lots of other bits and pieces, such as bird-feathers, shells, rocks, the skull of a dog, and so on. These things wouldn't mean much to anyone else perhaps, but for me they all have associations that I find it helpful to remember.

Sometimes I will just sit looking at the shrine for a while before I begin to meditate, just allowing the shrine to remind me why I'm there in front of it. Your practice of being more mindful can begin before you start the formal meditation. You can take care in the way you light the candles and incense, and try to be mindful of the movement of your body as you sit down.

Establish a routine that prepares you to meditate once you are on the cushion. Take time to make sure you are sitting as well as you can. Then spend a few minutes, or longer if needed, becoming aware of the body, giving it time to settle down and relax; a short body meditation is nearly always a good idea. Then just check in with yourself, becoming as conscious as you can of how you feel. This does not mean you have to analyse or cross-examine yourself; it just means giving yourself a chance to catch up with your state of mind. What is your general tone? Are you happy or sad, dull or bright? – this kind of thing.

Once you have a sense of yourself you should be as clear as possible about your intention. In some ways intention is the most important factor in supporting a productive meditation practice. It means simply knowing what you intend to do and why you are doing it. It sounds very simple, but over the years of teaching, and through my own experience, I have come to realize that it is easy to overlook it completely.

Decide what practice you are going to do, and remind yourself what that practice is aiming to do. Say to yourself 'I will do the Metta Bhavana; this practice helps me to develop loving-kindness.' Be clear. Many hours of sitting are wasted because people go into a meditation not knowing what they want to do. They keep switching from one practice to the other, and never really engaging in either.

There might now and then be times when you really feel you just want to sit without doing any formal practice. That's fine, but be clear about that too. On the whole, we do need the structure of a particular practice, otherwise we just drift. But now and then it can be good, particularly if you have been doing a fair amount of meditation, to just sit. In fact 'just sitting', as we call it, is a very difficult practice. It leaves a lot of room for distraction, and there is not much for the mind to focus on.

So remember the word intention. If you sit with intention – even if you feel that the meditation is not really going anywhere – it will have an effect. Just having the intention to develop positive states will spill over into your everyday life, even when you feel you are not making much progress in the practice itself. I really cannot over-emphasize this, so I will say it again: sit with an intention. This does not mean gritting your teeth. It means simply reminding yourself at the beginning of the practice of what you are doing, and reminding yourself again during the practice when you get distracted. If you just do that you will be doing all right.

Once you know what you intend to do, set your mind on the task, looking for the emotional energy to support you to do it. Acknowledge any resistance you might feel, then just go for it as wholeheartedly as you can, but without forcing it.

It is a good idea to decide for how long you are going to sit and stick to it. Even if it's difficult, carry on sitting for that length of time; try just to stay with it. If the practice is going really well, of course, feel free to extend it, but set yourself a minimum period, say fifteen to twenty minutes including preparation. It's a mistake to overdo it; much better to set yourself something you feel comfortable with. As you gain experience and get used to sitting, you will find that you will want to meditate for longer; but if you overdo it to start with and do not enjoy the practice, you may just build up negative associations with meditation and you'll find it difficult to sustain a practice over time.

As a rule, it is better to do a short meditation every day – even just ten minutes – than a longer one every few days. Meditation seems to have a cumulative effect, so consistency is preferable to whimsical bursts of enthusiasm. That said, don't be too rigid about this to start with. It took me a year before I had a fairly consistent daily practice. Try not to set yourself up to feel guilty if you do not make it to the cushion every day. Guilt is not a useful ally if you want enjoyment to make an entrance at some point.

The most common question I get asked by beginners to meditation is 'How do I know how long I have been meditating for?' The answer is, rather prosaically, 'Look at your watch.' If you really feel that looking at a clock will be too distracting, you could perhaps set a timer, not too loud, or even record a blank tape with a bell at five- or ten-minute intervals. But a watch placed on the floor in front of you, so you can half open your eyes and see the time, works just fine.

To begin with, at least, it's best to spend an equal amount of time on each of the stages of whichever meditation you have chosen, until you get a good feel for the practices. After a while, progress through the meditation can be a bit more flexible if you wish. In the Mindfulness of Breathing, in particular, you need to feel a little more concentrated before you move to the next stage, as it's a slightly finer object that you are using to focus on. So you may want to linger over the earlier stages if you are distracted – or pass over them more swiftly if you are soon quite concentrated.

In general, alternate the two practices. One will seem easier than the other, but it's still best to do them both regularly, as they complement and feed into each other. Again, you don't have to be too rigid, but bear in mind the possibility that the meditation you are having difficulty with is the one that is having the deepest impact.

As for when is the best time to meditate, there is no single answer to this. Most people find it easiest to meditate in the morning, and I certainly like to sit fairly soon after I have woken up. Other people need a cup of tea first. Morning meditation has the advantage of starting the day in a positive way, and it is often easiest to create the time for meditation then – you just get up a little earlier.

For some people, though, mornings just don't seem to work. If you feel like that, try meditating before you go to bed, but don't leave it until you are feeling sleepy. Meditating before bedtime may even help if you suffer from insomnia. In general, it is best if you can find a time that is good for you and keep to it. Often when we say to ourselves 'I will meditate later' we never quite get round to it – another reason why mornings are good.

What you want to avoid is thinking of meditation as a chore, and feeling bad if you don't do it. You aren't going to be kept in after school because you haven't done your homework. At its worst, meditation is always interesting and will repay us for our efforts. If you think you just don't have time, it's worth remembering that in the long term a regular practice will create more time for you, as you will find it easier to apply yourself to other activities. You might even find that you don't feel you have to do so much, that a lot of what you 'have' to do is unimportant in the larger scheme of things.

Maintaining your Practice

Although I don't have any way of knowing, I suspect that rather a low percentage of the very many people to whom I've taught meditation over the years are still finding their way to the cushion on anything like a regular basis, if at all. Although we might have had direct experience of the beneficial effects of meditation, it can still be difficult for most of us to maintain a regular practice. This is at first sight rather hard to understand. We know through our own experience that meditation can work, in the sense that it can allow us to achieve more positive states of mind. Surely this is what we want?

However, meditation is a challenge to the way we see ourselves. In particular, it challenges us to take fuller responsibility for our lives. It challenges us to acknowledge that we are responsible for how we feel, and for the way in which we lead our life.

This might feel quite uncomfortable, as over a long time we have tended to come up with reasons why we are as we are, reasons why our life is how it is; and often these reasons relate to factors outside of ourselves – our work, our family, other people, and so on. We attribute to these outside factors a lot of power over our well-being and happiness, either in the present or in the wished-for future.

Meditation to some degree stands this way of thinking on its head. It is not so much that the outside world works upon us to determine our fate. It is much more as though we create the outside world quite directly through our own mental states. Meditation helps us to see that the way we view the world is not objective, but that we create our own version of the world.

Often we have created a version that leaves us feeling passive, even a victim of external circumstances. This is not to say that the outside world is subjective; only that our experience of it is subjective. Meditation works against this subjective view of the world, in that we begin to bring fewer 'ideas' to the world; our awareness becomes cleaner.

We are very attached to our version of the world, and it might well be difficult for us to give up the views and prejudices we have. Our sense of who we are is closely bound up with the way we see things, and it would be unrealistic to think that we can effortlessly give up views that have been conditioning us – essentially creating us – over many years. While we might like the idea of breaking out of the limiting ways we look at our lives, in reality it is frightening to give them up.

So to some extent we are all resistant to change. We all have a tendency to cling to what we know, even if it isn't very positive. We don't want to see that our lives are in our own hands to a far greater degree than most of us ever experience. Over time, the meditations will equip us for change, giving us the awareness to see more clearly what we need to change, and giving us the courage to make those changes.

However, this will take a while, and in the meantime there is often a period where it might feel as though meditation is making our lives harder. We are being faced more clearly with how we limit ourselves, but we have not quite reached the point where we can make the necessary changes. The problem is that we can't see meditation as just another activity we can perform to enhance our lives. When our practice begins to bite it will change our lives. In the end we all have to decide if we are prepared for our lives to change in what can often be quite dramatic ways.

We are meditating because we want to feel different in some way, but we do not always make the connection between feeling different and being different. If we want change to come about we have to be prepared to change. This means we will have to let go of the attitudes towards ourselves and others that keep us how we are. While there is a great sense of liberation in letting go of attitudes which cut us off from others, in dropping views of ourselves which restrict our creativity, it is not necessarily an easy process. It can sometimes seem a whole lot easier to turn on the television and have a beer – to keep to the well-worn habits that define and confine us.

We can of course approach the two practices we have learned just as a means of relaxation, of calming down the chatter of the mind. Certainly, this is an important purpose of them both. But in the long term I don't think this will prove to be very sustaining. In fact, even if we have strong meditation experiences, even if we achieve very positive mental states – this alone will not, after a while, be enough to keep us practising.

For most of us the implications of a regular practice are too far-reaching for us to cope with, outside of a more general context of support and encouragement from others who are also practising. One of the real joys of meditation for me is that it has brought me into contact with other people who meditate, who feel it is worth while to try to change who and what they are, people with some degree of vision. Meditation attracts people of all types; what they have in common is a sense that positive change is possible.

Let's look a bit more at the pressures that our practice can put upon the patterns of our lives – and the way these conflicts are resolved. We are meditating in the first place because we are unfulfilled in some way. Say our job makes us really tense – we take up meditation to counteract this. What then happens is that we begin to experience more and more clearly the elements in our work that cause this tension.

The thing is that meditation is not like a pill that makes us more relaxed or happier. It is a means by which, through our own efforts, we bring about change in our mental states. This means that the factors in our life that cause us to feel bad become less and less acceptable to us. Now it may seem that I have contradicted myself: what has happened to the idea that we create the quality of the outside world with our mental states? In fact it is of course a two-way process.

When we are meditating we can control the conditions we are in. In the everyday world we can't. Of course, to some extent meditation makes us less susceptible to these external conditions, because we have found a source of positivity within ourselves. But in another way it also makes us less willing to tolerate negative conditions for long periods of time if we don't have to.

If we are in a generally dull and negative state, negative external conditions will sustain that state; and in a sense they will not bother us too much because they match our mental state. However, if we are managing to create bright positive states through meditation we will find the forces pulling us back down very difficult to put up with. We have started to realize that we need not be stuck with the habits of mind that give us grief; and it's a natural step then to realize that we need not be stuck with patterns of living in the world that give us or others grief either. We are creating a conflict that at some point we will be forced to resolve.

This is the nature of spiritual growth. Our meditation brings us into conflict with the realities of our life, so we have to change the external or internal conditions to be in harmony with our meditation. Now what normally happens is the opposite: we resolve this conflict by dropping the meditation. People will often say 'Yes, it really seemed to help for a while, and then I kind of just stopped doing it.'

We stop doing it when it begins to bite, when it begins to challenge the patterns of our life. It is very difficult for this not to happen unless we have a broader context that supports the parts of us that want to change. Meditation is not about being happier with our lot; it is about becoming more and more creatively active in our life and the world around us. Increased awareness and kindness demands an expression in the concrete world. If we really feel metta when we encounter suffering we will feel the arising of compassion, a desire – that is more like a decision – to alleviate this suffering.

Without the support and encouragement of others the path of meditation is a very difficult one. Without the support of ideas and ethical guidelines, our practice is not grounded and connected with the world and everyday life. It is for this reason that Buddhism puts such a strong emphasis on the spiritual community and also on the understanding of some basic ideas that underpin our intention to change. We will look at some elements of Buddhist ethics in the next chapter.

Perhaps I am wrong – it may be that many of the people I have taught to meditate are still doing so, day after day, on their cushions in their own homes. I very much hope this is the case. But I think that most of those who are keeping up a meditation practice are part of some kind of spiritual community. They have found support for their endeavours. This might be a formal group or just a loose association of friends, but they have some sense of developing with others.

Although meditation is something we do alone, it thrives on a human context. To meditate now and then with a group is of great benefit and has a different feel to solo practice. By their very nature the qualities we are trying to develop need to be shared. To share them with others who we know are also attempting to develop them is a sustaining joy.

twelve

MEDITATION AND ETHICS

I hope it is becoming clear that meditation is not a clip-on gadget for making life meaningful. Although we employ simple techniques to help us, meditation is not a technique but a process of becoming aware. That is meditation.

'I am the husband of Marge, I work at the nuclear power plant, I have two children.' Instead of this, we have a direct experience of who we are. This is me now, feeling happy, feeling sad, unable to count to ten breaths without being distracted. We have created a space in our lives to experience the results of all the other things that we do. When I stop doing, this is me, this is the effect that my life is having on me.

So we begin to get more realistic about ourselves, we begin to see that much of the time we are confused, rushing around, being somebody who is very often not much like the real us anyway. It's as though what we are doing isn't really us, it's just something we have to do. The real us is keeping its head down, waiting its chance. Maybe it will pop out now and then, on vacation perhaps. Sometimes the real us has not got very much to do with our life.

It was not until I was in my late twenties that I came across poetry. It had nothing to do with my life before then. I was not brought up in a situation where it existed, and none of my friends were interested in it. But there it was, waiting to be found. I had an idea about myself that didn't allow the possibility that I might love poetry. Then I found it and it was nearer to the real me than anything else I had ever discovered. In meditation we are trying to give this real us a kind of fighting chance to get out there and strut its stuff a bit.

Of course, this is just a way of speaking, because the truth is that the real us is ordinary old everyday us. The 'real' us that never comes out is just a fantasy. Maybe we have a dream of how we would like to be, given the chance. But no one is going to give us that chance. Life is not like that. We have to take our own chances.

When we meditate we begin to create a kind of opposing force in our lives to the force of our actions, our activities. We introduce the force of no-action, non-activity. The Chinese Zen master, Josho, was once passing by the main hall of the monastery of which he was the abbot, and saw a monk worshipping. So Josho hit him with his stick. The monk protested, saying, 'After all, worshipping is a good thing,' to which Josho replied, 'A good thing isn't as good as nothing.'

What will happen eventually is that the kind of clarity we have in meditation is continued over into the rest of our lives. When that happens there will be no difference between our everyday mind and our meditative mind. But at the moment and for a while to come there is a difference. Ethics in Buddhism is a way of trying to bring the rest of our lives into line with meditation.

So here we have a bit of a turnaround. We do not meditate to help our life; our life outside meditation becomes a way of helping our meditation. This is because what we are in our practice is nearer to what we really are. So we introduce ideas into our life which can help us be more in tune with this truer self. The idea of ethics in

Buddhism is to offer a model of how we would act if we were in touch with the best of ourselves all the time.

In a sense, there is only one ethic in Buddhism, and all the others come out of it. It is the principle of non-harm towards all living beings and the cultivation of loving-kindness towards all living beings. Anything we do that fits into that guideline is regarded as 'skilful'; while anything that does not is regarded as 'unskilful'. In other words, a skilful action is based in kindness and clarity; an unskilful one in states of greed or hatred or ignorance.

When we act in an unskilful way it causes our mind to become disturbed, and when we sit down to meditate we have to deal with this disturbed mind. We have to make a big effort to restore some sense of balance and calm to the mind. Now we might not have done anything 'bad', but we feel disturbed. This is because actions in the Buddhist sense of the word are of three kinds: they can be actions of the body, of speech, or of mind. So we didn't hit anyone, we didn't even shout at them, but we wished them dead. This is an action of the mind.

Now it isn't too hard to control the body, and it's not impossible to control our speech, but it is very hard indeed to control the mind. This is because the mind is on the whole very dull and predictable. If the last time we couldn't find the other sock we felt annoyed, swore, and kicked the drawer, well, the chances are pretty good that the next time it happens we will perform the same sort of routine. Nothing so awful about that, except that it shows what a dull kind of mind we have. It would nearly always like to do the same thing over and over – have the same negative reactions, think the same negative thoughts.

When we meditate we see the dullness of the mind, doing the same old stuff again and again. This is really the beginning, because we then want to do something new, something more interesting and exciting with the mind. When we behave ethically we check our minds from going into their old routine and try to find something new to do. We can begin that on the cushion but soon we will want to take it out into the rest of our lives, so that our meditation is more enjoyable.

Buddhism tells us that actions have consequences – we become our actions, we are our habits. When we act in a certain way we encourage the habit of mind that was the 'emotion' behind that action. In meditation we begin to see, to feel, the emotions behind our actions, and we also deliberately encourage positive emotion that will lead to positive action. So ethical behaviour is behaviour that supports positive emotion. We work on our mental states directly when we meditate. When we act with kindness and clarity we are also working on our mental states, as these actions will encourage positive emotions.

Meditation gives us the awareness to act more creatively, which in turn reinforces the emotional state behind the act and fuels further positive action. The same thing works in reverse. So ethics in Buddhism give us objective guidelines that help us to understand what actions lead to and encourage positive rather than negative mental states.

While it is not within the scope of this book to look in any detail at Buddhist ethics, I would just like to mention the five basic ethical guidelines of the Buddhist tradition. With a little reflection we will be able to see to what degree our lives conform to these principles, and therefore see to what extent we are creating the conditions for the arising of either positive or negative mental states.

These guidelines are known as the five precepts. A precept is a training principle – i.e. what we need to do in order to develop spiritually, to develop as a human being. They can be formulated either in terms of what to do, or in terms of what to avoid doing. Here they are in both formulations:

With deeds of loving kindness, I purify my body.
I undertake to abstain from taking life.

With open-handed generosity, I purify my body.
I undertake to abstain from taking the not-given.

With stillness, simplicity, and contentment, I purify my body.
I undertake to abstain from sexual misconduct.

With truthful communication, I purify my speech.
I undertake to abstain from false speech.

With mindfulness clear and radiant, I purify my mind.
I undertake to abstain from taking intoxicants.

It is important to try to see these not as rules, but as expressions of positive mental/emotional states; and as comprising a guide to the kinds of actions that support the development of such states. Our understanding of the precepts is not a static thing. As we change, we see more deeply into the emotional state that each precept encourages and the implications of that emotional state.

For example, if we look at the first precept we might think, 'Oh, at least I'm all right there, I haven't killed anyone lately.' But it should be easy to see that this precept also relates to causing suffering in less direct ways – and to the taking of non-human life. It relates to the way we treat the world around us. Do our financial investments support the careless exploitation of others or the environment? Does our work cause suffering in some way? With a little reflection we can expand these precepts out into all aspects of our lives.

It is very hard indeed to follow the precepts perfectly. In fact, it is said that only a fully Enlightened person can do so, because only when we are fully Enlightened are we completely free from greed, hatred, and delusion, which are what fuel unskilful action. So we undertake the precepts as a means of training; we do our best to follow them, and, even more importantly, we do our best to understand how going against them leads to unhappiness and suffering for ourselves and others.

It is our state of mind which determines the quality of our lives. Meditation is not a means of removing ourselves from the harshness of the world around us, but rather a way of equipping ourselves with the internal resources to respond creatively to the real world. To act creatively does not mean we have to do something special. It means that in our everyday lives we try to relate from what is best in us, we try to live by what is really important to us. As Socrates rather bluntly puts it, 'The unexamined life is not worth living.'

thirteen

WHY MEDITATE?

Within this book I have concentrated on meditation as a means of developing increasingly positive mental states, and to a lesser degree I have introduced the idea of insight – in a preliminary way at least. But if I sit down and think about why I practise, it is not actually because of either of these two things. That is not to say that they are not important to me. They are, and they certainly play some part in motivating me.

But there is something else that seems more fundamental, and that is simply the experience of meditation itself. By this I do not mean the experience of a 'good' meditation. I am not talking about the great pleasure that sometimes arises from meditation – no, I am just saying that the fact of meditating, however that might be, is the reason I do it.

However we live, our lives are, in a sense, a search to find ourselves, to become aware of what and who we are. Much of this searching is done in the world outside; it is in relationship to other people, it is in relationship to the challenges the world brings up for us. We change and learn from these interactions, and in these ways our character is formed. Besides, there is much joy and wonder in the world and in others. But however rich and rewarding our life might be, there is a certain experience of ourselves that is not gained through such interaction.

Sitting quietly, watching our own mind, is the simplest thing we can do. By this I mean it is the purest expression of what we are. Whatever we do expresses our nature in some way or other; how we walk, how we talk – we cannot do anything that is not an expression of our own nature. But any activity in this sense is quite complicated; even in something as simple as walking, there is a lot going on, a lot to be aware of.

When we meditate we cut down what is happening to its bare essentials. There is just us. In this sense, when we sit for meditation we leave the world, we even leave time. When we meditate there is not any future or past – or rather they are both contained in the present. In this sense again, when we meditate we are not even concerned with achieving a certain state. Just by meditating we are doing all that we need to do. We are with ourselves in the simplest way we can be, and so we experience ourselves at the deepest level.

This does not mean we have a profound experience of ourselves necessarily. Maybe we just feel unhappy or angry. This is what we experience. So we are willing to sit quietly feeling unhappy. We don't want to get up and phone a friend – maybe we will do that later. But for now we just sit. When we can do this – and we can do it if we choose – we have complete freedom. We are no longer in the grip of emotions: we feel them very deeply; we are happy, or we are sad, but that is just it. Somehow we do not add anything else to these feelings. We do not say 'I am sad – I must do something, I must cheer up; I must get drunk.' It is enough that I am sad and that this is how it is.

When someone is very depressed or maybe when someone is dying, there is sometimes nothing we can do for them. There is no way we can change what is happening for them. But there is a way of being with people in these sorts of situations where you are just with them. You are not adding anything to or taking anything away from the situation, and yet you are there; you are part of the situation. And although you can do nothing you can witness it. I am not talking here about making the situation better for the other person. Maybe you can, but that is not what I am talking about. I am talking about just being able to be in that situation without having to change it, or being able to.

Maybe you are thinking, 'Well, what is the point of that? Big deal.' But it seems to me vital that we develop the ability to do this. To be with what is. In the end this is what meditation is about for me, this being with myself – not for any reason, not in order to change anything, but just to witness myself.

My hut lies in the middle of a dense forest;
Every year the green ivy grows longer.
No news of the affairs of men,
Only the occasional song of a wood cutter.
The sun shines and I mend my robe;
When the moon comes out I read Buddhist poems.
I have nothing to report, my friends.
If you want to find the meaning, stop chasing after so many things.

Conclusion

We all come to meditation with our own reasons, with a feeling that perhaps meditation can help us in some way. Few of us really understand what it is that we are embarking on. Our reasons for meditating may be simply to feel more relaxed, to enjoy life to a greater degree. And this is where we start from. However, if we allow it, meditation can be the beginning of life's greatest challenge and adventure.

We see that in fact there is no ceiling on what we can become other than the one we put there ourselves. Even early on we can catch a glimpse of what we can be. We can experience ourselves in a completely new way. We gain some sense that we can be free from negative states, and free to act creatively in the world.

However, if we embark on the path of self-transformation, we soon learn that it is a long path and in many ways a difficult path. We will find that we need others to support our efforts, others who also feel that this path is the only one really worth treading.

We might find that many people cannot understand what we are doing, and see it as some form of escapism. Others feel uneasy with talk of spiritual change, with the idea of conscious transformation of the mind. This is largely due to the fact that spiritual longing, a wish to be more fully ourselves, is inherent in the human being, and many people feel threatened because they have a sense that they have denied this aspect of themselves.

But there are others out there who have not denied what is the most basic longing of the human heart. If you can find others who also meditate, who have a desire to develop, they will be a great support for your practice, so see if you can find a group to meditate with. If there isn't one around, you might want to think about trying to start your own.

We are told that after the Buddha gained Enlightenment he was at first reluctant to teach, as he did not think what he had experienced could be communicated. Then he had a great vision; it was a vision of the whole of humanity as a vast field of lotuses. He saw that while many of the lotuses were still firmly stuck in the mud, others were pushing to the surface of the water, while still others were beginning to bud or even coming into bloom.

In other words, he saw that there were others to share his experience with. Buddhism is the path to the very same experience that the Buddha had. The Buddhist way is the way to freedom. It is the path that some men and women of all cultures and at all times have valued, not just under the name of Buddhism, but under many names, wherever an individual has had a sincere desire to develop awareness and kindness, has had a sincere desire to be truly human, and has put this desire into practice. There the path of freedom has been found.

We are particularly lucky, for although in our culture this path is not in general highly valued, we also live at a time where there is greater access to the support and help that we need to tread the way of freedom. In particular, I believe that Buddhism and Buddhist practices offer a great opportunity for us to become what in our hearts we know we have to become, to become what we really are.

Meditation is the first step on this path. It is the simple and natural process of beginning to take the time to get to know ourselves, beginning to cultivate what is best in ourselves. It is a means by which we can slowly uncover what is highest in us, and open up more and more to the beauty all around us. Good luck.

IN BEAUTY MAY I WALK

In beauty	may I walk
All day long	may I walk
Through the returning seasons	may I walk
Beautifully will I possess again	
Beautifully birds	
Beautifully joyful birds	

On the trail marked with pollen   may I walk
With grasshoppers about my feet   may I walk
With dew about my feet   may I walk
With beauty   may I walk
With beauty before me   may I walk
With beauty behind me   may I walk
With beauty above me   may I walk
With beauty all around me   may I walk
In old age, wandering on a trail of beauty,
                   lively,   may I walk
In old age, wandering on a trail of beauty,
             living again,   may I walk
It is finished in beauty
It is finished in beauty

Index

The Windhorse symbolizes the energy of the enlightened mind carrying the Three Jewels – the Buddha, the Dharma, and the Sangha – to all sentient beings.

Buddhism is one of the fastest growing spiritual traditions in the Western world. Throughout its 2,500-year history, it has always succeeded in adapting its mode of expression to suit whatever culture it has encountered.

Windhorse Publications aims to continue this tradition as Buddhism comes to the West. Today's Westerners are heirs to the entire Buddhist tradition, free to draw instruction and inspiration from all the many schools and branches. Windhorse publishes works by authors who not only understand the Buddhist tradition but are also familiar with Western culture and the Western mind.

For orders and catalogues contact:

WINDHORSE PUBLICATIONS	WINDHORSE BOOKS	CONSORTIUM INC
11 PARK ROAD	PO BOX 574	P O BOX 574
BIRMINGHAM	NEWTON NSW 2042	ST PAUL MN 55114
B13 8AB	AUSTRALIA	USA
UK		

Windhorse Publications is an arm of the Friends of the Western Buddhist Order, which has more than sixty centres on five continents. Through these centres, members of the Western Buddhist Order offer regular programmes of events for the general public and for more experienced students. These include meditation classes, public talks, study on Buddhist themes and texts, and 'bodywork' classes such as t'ai chi, yoga, and massage. The FWBO also runs several retreat centres and the Karuna Trust, a fundraising charity that supports social welfare projects in the slums and villages of India.

Many FWBO centres have residential spiritual communities and ethical businesses associated with them. Arts activities are encouraged too, as is the development of strong bonds of friendship between people who share the same ideals. In this way the FWBO is developing a unique approach to Buddhism, not simply as a set of techniques, less still as an exotic cultural interest, but as a creatively directed way of life for people living in the modern world. If you would like more information about the FWBO please write to:

LONDON BUDDHIST CENTRE   ARYALOKA
51 ROMAN ROAD   HEARTWOOD CIRCLE
LONDON   NEWMARKET
E2 0HU   NEW HAMPSHIRE
UK   NH 03857   USA

ALSO FROM WINDHORSE PUBLICATIONS

WILDMIND:

A STEP-BY-STEP GUIDE TO MEDITATION

by Bodhipaksa

A Wildmind is as spacious as a clear blue sky, as still as a lake at dawn; such a mind is a source of richness and fulfilment. It is a mind that is free, spontaneous, and abundantly creative. It is a place we can spend the rest of our lives exploring.

Buddhist meditation teacher Bodhipaksa shows us how we can use simple meditation practices to realize the potential of our minds and hearts, freeing ourselves from restrictive habits and fears and developing a more loving heart and a clearer mind. Drawn from the very successful online meditation website, www.wildmind.org, it is written in short sections to encourage reflection and for practices to 'sink in'.

256 pages, with photographs
ISBN 1 899579 55 9
£11.99/$18.95/€18.95

INTRODUCING BUDDHISM

by Chris Pauling

The best-selling *Introducing Buddhism* is a lively and engaging guide for Westerners who want to learn more about Buddhism as a path of spiritual growth.

Written in a clear, informal style, it explains the essential teachings and practices on which all mainstream Buddhists agree, focusing on ethics, meditation, and wisdom. *Introducing Buddhism* shows how this ancient wisdom is more than ever relevant to the psychological, social, and spiritual issues concerning men and women in the West today.

80 pages
ISBN 0 904766 97 7
£4.99/$8.95/€8.95

THE BREATH
by Vessantara

This is an incredibly useful combination of practical instruction on the mindfulness of breathing with much broader lessons on where the breath can lead us. Vessantara, a meditator of many years experience, offers us:

- Clear instruction on how to meditate on the breath
- Practical ways to integrate meditation into our lives
- Suggestions for deepening calm and concentration
- Advice on how to let go and dive into experience
- Insights into the lessons of the breath

144 pages
ISBN 1 899579 69 9
£6.99/$10.99/€10.99

THE HEART
by Vessantara

(forthcoming, summer 2006)
Explore the potential of your heart – and discover a warmer, more loving you.

Cultivating more warmth, more kindness, more happiness is possible for all of us. Through the loving-kindness meditation, the gentle and encouraging approach of experienced meditator Vessantara helps us to discover the positive wonder of what is already in our hearts. Accessible for those new to or experienced in meditation as well as teachers, it provides clear instruction with suggestions for integrating meditation and what we can learn from it into our lives.

144 pages
ISBN 1 899579 71 0
£6.99/$10.99/€10.99

THE BUDDHIST PATH TO AWAKENING
by Tejananda

A straightforward and encouraging introduction to the path of the Buddha and his followers, *The Buddhist Path to Awakening* covers the Four Noble Truths, the Threefold Path, the Three Jewels, and much more.

Tejananda alerts us to the Buddha's wake-up call to 'awaken' to the joy and reality of life around us, illustrating how the Buddhist path can help us develop a clearer mind and a more compassionate heart.

224 pages, with diagrams
ISBN 1 899579 02 8
£8.99/$14.95/€14.95

WHAT IS THE DHARMA?
THE ESSENTIAL TEACHINGS OF THE BUDDHA
by Sangharakshita

To walk in the footsteps of the Buddha we need a clear and thorough guide to the essential principles of Buddhism. Whether we have just begun our journey or are practitioners with more experience, *What is the Dharma?* is an indispensable exploration of the Buddha's teachings as found in the main Buddhist traditions.

Constantly returning to the question 'How can this help me?' Sangharakshita examines a variety of fundamental principles, including: karma and rebirth, nirvana and shunyata, conditioned co-production, impermanence, unsatisfactoriness and insubstantiality, ethics, meditation, and wisdom.

The result is a refreshing, unsettling, and inspiring book that lays before us the essential Dharma, timeless and universal.

272 pages
ISBN 1 899579 01 X
£9.99/$16.95/€16.95

LIVING WITH AWARENESS:
A GUIDE TO THE SATIPATTHANA SUTTA
by Sangharakshita

Paying attention to how things look, sound, and feel makes them more enjoyable; it is as simple (and as difficult) as that.

Mindfulness and the breath – this deceptively simple yet profound teaching in the *Satipatthana Sutta* is the basis of much insight meditation practice today. By looking at aspects of our daily life, such as Remembering, Looking, Dying, Reflecting, Sangharakshita shows how broad an application the practice of mindfulness can have – and how our experience can be enriched by its presence.

200 pages
ISBN 1 899579 38 9
£11.99/$17.95/€17.95

LIVING WITH KINDNESS:
THE BUDDHA'S TEACHING ON METTA
by Sangharakshita

'Just as a mother would protect her only child at the risk of her own life, let thoughts of boundless love pervade the whole world.' Karaniya Metta Sutta

Kindness is one of the most basic qualities we can possess, and one of the most powerful. In Buddhism it is called metta – an opening of the heart to all that we meet. This book takes us step by step through the Buddha's words in the *Karaniya Metta Sutta* to consider its meaning, its ethical foundations, and its cultivation, culmination, and realization. Excellent for beginners and an insightful refresher for those looking for another way to engage with metta.

160 pages
ISBN 1 899579 64 8
£9.99/$14.95/€14.95

MEDITATION:
THE BUDDHIST WAY OF TRANQUILLITY AND
INSIGHT

by Kamalashila

This is a truly practical guide to read, enjoy and use. A great addition to the meditator's bookshelf. **Yoga and Health**

A clear and comprehensive handbook of Buddhist meditation for both beginners and the more experienced – what meditation is and where it might take us. This book covers all you need to know on how to establish a meditation practice, as well as helpful advice and greater detail for those wishing to deepen their experience of meditation. Complete with photographs, charts, and diagrams.

304 pages, with charts and illustrations
ISBN 1 899579 05 2
£13.99/$21.95/€21.95

MEETING THE BUDDHAS:
A GUIDE TO THE BUDDHAS, BODHISATTVAS, AND
TANTRIC DEITIES

by Vessantara

A mysterious, serene smile lights the face of the Buddha. Wild-haired women dance in the flames of freedom. Buddhism speaks not only to the rational mind, but to the emotions and the imagination through myths, symbols, colour and sound.

This best-selling book invites us on a vivid and inspiring journey to the magical heart of Buddhist visualization and devotional practices. With Vessantara as our experienced guide we are introduced to the main Buddhas, Bodhisattvas, and Tantric deities we may be fortunate to meet in that miraculous realm. A unique resource to be referred to again and again.

368 pages, with text illustrations and colour plates
ISBN 0 904766 53 5
£16.99/$27.95/€27.95

COME AND SEE FOR YOURSELF:
THE BUDDHIST PATH TO HAPPINESS
by Ayya Khema

When we stop searching for happiness in the world and look to the depths of meditation instead, we discover that we carry within ourselves everything for which we have been searching.

Ayya Khema, the first Western woman to become a Theravadin Buddhist nun, was highly regarded for the depth and sincerity of her practice.

Here she explores twelve short extracts from the vast collection of Buddhist teachings, encouraging us to take an honest look at ourselves and discover that elusive happiness for which we search.

208 pages
ISBN 1 899579 45 1
£9.99/$15.95/€15.95

TALES OF FREEDOM:
WISDOM FROM THE BUDDHIST TRADITION
by Vessantara

Stories have the power to transform us as we enter their world. Drawn from the rich variety of the Buddhist tradition, these beautifully-told stories convey a sense of inner freedom. We see ordinary people liberate themselves from anger and grief, and great teachers remain free even in the face of death. Vessantara's commentary shows us how we can move towards that freedom in our own lives.

A clear-sighted, lucid, and immensely enjoyable journey through Buddhist teachings which will be of enormous benefit to Buddhists and non- Buddhists alike. I loved this book.

Mick Brown, author of *The Spiritual Tourist*

216 pages
ISBN 1 899579 27 3
£9.99/$16.95/€16.95

WRITING YOUR WAY
by Manjusvara (David Keefe)

It's about learning how to unlock your creativity, how to let language work through you and begin dancing across the page.

Emerging out of the Wolf at the Door writing workshops taught worldwide, *Writing Your Way* helps us to see writing as a transformative tool in our search for wholeness. Manjusvara (David Keefe) expertly guides us to the heart of writing as well as to aspects of Buddhism, with exercises that delicately weave in teachings on mindfulness and compassion, freedom and openness.

Contains more good advice about writing than any other book I have read.

Robert Gray, award-winning poet and creative writing teacher

160 pages
ISBN 1 899579 67 2
£8.99/$12.95/€12.95

DETOX YOUR HEART
by Valerie Mason-John

Passes on the wisdom of hard experience and shows there is a way to get yourself back on track

Jenni Murray, BBC's Women's Hour

Offers readers both the inspiration and the insight to work on themselves

Christopher Titmuss, author of *Transforming Our Terror*

Have you ever felt angry, resnetful, or even revengeful? The author draws on her own life, personal stories, and her work as an anger management trainer to explore why we experience such emotions and how we can transform toxins like anger, hatred, and fear.

Our ability to love and be open is often blocked by jealousy, hatred, anger, prejudice, fear, resentment. With short exercises drawing on Buddhist teachings that encourage pausing, connecting, feeling, and loving, *Detox Your Heart* helps us to renew and open our heart.

208 pages
ISBN 1899579 65 6
£9.99/$13.95/€13.95

EXPLORING KARMA & REBIRTH

by Nagapriya

Every Buddhist should read it **David Loy**

An excellent introduction **Stephen Batchelor**

Cogent, knowledgeable, and penetrating **Norman Fischer**

Exploring Karma & Rebirth helps us to unravel the complexities of these two important but often misunderstood Buddhist doctrines. Clarifying, examining and considering them, it offers an imaginative reading of what the teachings could mean for us now. Both informative and thought provoking, above all, *Exploring Karma & Rebirth* insists that, to be of enduring value, these doctrines must continue to serve the overriding aim of Buddhism: spiritual awakening.

176 pages

ISBN 1 899579 61 3

£8.99/$13.95/€13.95

PRINCIPLES OF BUDDHISM

by Kulananda

Buddhism is one of the most popular religions of today – its teachings on kindness, simplicity, and interconnectedness are attracting many people disenchanted with the world's all-pervading consumerism.

This simple guide holds the essential teachings and methods of practice to help bring these qualities alive. Going back to the roots of Buddhism, it highlights and explains:

- the central ideas and beliefs of Buddhism
- karma and rebirth
- meditation
- Buddhism in the world today

The author, Kulananda, a practising Buddhist for 30 years, shows us how this approach to life can make a real difference to us and our capacity to grow clearer, wiser, and happier.

160 pages

ISBN 1 899579 59 1

£5.99/$8.95/€8.95